Knit It!

Knit It!

LEARN THE BASICS *and* KNIT 22 BEAUTIFUL PROJECTS

Melissa Leapman

Photographs by Alexandra Grablewski

CHRONICLE BOOKS
SAN FRANCISCO

for JOAN MURPHY,
knitter extraordinaire

Text and illustrations copyright © 2014
by Melissa Leapman.

Photographs copyright © 2014
by Alexandra Grablewski.

Library of Congress
Cataloging-in-Publication Data:

Leapman, Melissa.

Knit it! : learn the basics and knit 22 beautiful
projects / Melissa Leapman.

    pages cm

ISBN 978-1-4521-2451-3

Includes bibliographical references and index.

1. Knitting. I. Title.

TT820.L3875 2014

746.43′2—dc23

                         2013037028

Manufactured in China

MIX
Paper from
responsible sources
FSC® C008047

Designed by Tracy Sunrize Johnson *and*
Hillary Caudle

10 9 8 7 6 5 4 3 2 1

Chronicle Books LLC
680 Second Street
San Francisco, California 94107
www.chroniclebooks.com

ACKNOWLEDGMENTS

I could not have completed this project without the help of many important people.

I am grateful to the following knitters for their help testing the patterns and creating the samples for this project: Karen Forbes, Nancy Harrington, Cheryl Keeley, Joan Murphy, Patty Olson, Jen Owens, Sarah Peasley, Debbie Prout, Debbie Radtke, Catherine Schiesz, Heather Start, Lauren Voeltz, and Marcia Weinert.

Special thanks go to my fabulous (and tireless!) project assistant for this book, Cindy Grosch. You ensured that the designs were camera-ready—and kept the author sane.

Thank you, Joni Conigio, for once again making me the luckiest author in the industry. Your beautiful work makes mine look better.

Just think: Together we'll be bringing lots of new knitters into the fold!

CONTENTS

INTRODUCTION

Knitting is a magical pastime.

Some folks consider it an art form. Others find it a practical and fun craft. For all, it is a technique that enables us to transform soft balls of yarn into beautiful and useful objects for ourselves and others.

Knitting has become incredibly popular in the past several years. Trendy hand knits are showing up everywhere: on the pages of leading fashion magazines, on the shelves of your favorite boutique, on fashion runways all over the world, and—if you could sneak a peek—in the models' own shopping bags.

The biggest surprise about knitting is how easy it is to learn. In fact, I taught myself as a kid in high school. With very little investment in tools and materials, you can have yarn and needles perched in your hands and be happily stitching away in no time!

Drawing on my experience teaching workshops to countless crafters, this book lays the groundwork for a lifetime of knitting—no prior skills necessary! Part 1 offers step-by-step instructions for the essential knitting know-how you'll

need from the moment you walk into a yarn shop to the day you wear your first hand-knit sweater. And, since even expert knitters make mistakes, I've included a useful section called I Goofed! Now What? (page 65) to help you fix inevitable errors.

Part 2 includes twenty-two projects that are easy—and fun—to knit. You'll find patterns for a variety of clothing, accessories, and home décor items, with plenty of options, whether you are knitting for yourself or the loved ones in your life. The projects are arranged in order to gradually add on to your skills as you work through the book. From the baby shower–friendly Color Me Mine throw (page 79) and the homey Pouf Positive (page 87) decorative floor pillow to the cozy Hat Trick (page 91) for men and the Get in Line sweater (page 101) for women, these projects will allow you to build your skills while knitting up unique items.

Each project includes a "Skill Set," which lists all the techniques necessary to complete the project. If something in the skill list looks unfamiliar, don't give up; just turn to the page referred to and learn something new. For absolute newbies, I'd suggest starting with Tie One On (page 71) or Taking a Ribbing (page 75). These simple projects will give you the confidence to keep knitting.

"Yarn," "Needles," and "Notions" for each pattern list all the tools and supplies you'll need to make the project. If you'd like your version to duplicate the one photographed, choose the specific yarn called for. You can use the Resources: Materials in the back of the book for a list of yarn companies; they can suggest yarn shops local to your area. As convenient as the Internet is for most things, I bet you'll want to select your yarn and colors in person. Knitting is a tactile sport: Choose yarn that makes you happy!

You'll notice that each pattern also includes a "Knitting Know-How" tip or two, where you'll discover my pro tips and tricks to help you build your skills—and your confidence. Remember that mastering a new motor skill like knitting can feel awkward at first. Be patient with yourself as you learn. Everyone was once a beginner.

Best of all, each project also includes a "Change It Up!" suggestion to help you customize and put your personal spin on the item, letting you create something new and different. If a shawl doesn't suit your lifestyle, you can easily adjust the Under Wraps shawl project (page 179) into a cozy afghan, for example. Knitting is always fun and stimulating. I hope it excites you as much as it does me.

Let's begin! We have the whole world of knitting to explore together.

Happy knitting!

PART 1: THE BASICS

THIS PART OF THE BOOK PRESENTS EVERYTHING YOU NEED TO KNOW TO GET STARTED KNITTING, FROM THE TOOLS AND MATERIALS YOU WILL USE TO ESSENTIAL STITCHES AND HOW TO READ A KNITTING PATTERN.

MATERIALS AND SUPPLIES

You only need a few fundamental materials to get started. Assemble the following items in your knitting bag.

YARN

Lucky for us, companies offer a fantastic array of yarns from all over the world, many of which can be found online. Before you start any project, be sure to read the yarn label, which contains important information.

FIBER CONTENT

Yarns can be made from all sorts of different fibers, from warm and cozy wools to silky cottons to workhorse machine-washable acrylics. Some yarns are blends of natural and man-made fibers and try to offer the best of both worlds. Since the way a knitted fabric feels is as important as how it looks, I suggest you experiment knitting with lots of different yarns to find the ones you love. If you haven't looked at yarns recently, you'll be amazed by the variety!

YARDAGE

This information tells you how much yarn is in the skein (a.k.a. the ball). It will help you determine how much yarn to purchase to make a specific project.

YARN WEIGHT

This describes the thickness of a single strand of the yarn. The Craft Yarn Council of America has set standard categories for yarn weights, from 1 (super fine) to 6 (super bulky). Bulky yarns knit up quickly with larger knitting needles and require less yarn yardage for the same size finished project.

SUGGESTED KNITTING GAUGE

Here's where the yarn manufacturer recommends a particular knitting needle size and how many stitches would usually result over 4 in/10 cm. The finer the yarn, the more stitches and rows are needed to create fabric of a particular size. Note that the needle size printed on the label is only a suggestion. All knitters, even seasoned ones, vary in how they knit and the needles they use to achieve the recommended gauge. And remember, the same yarn can be knit at one gauge for socks and at another gauge for a lacy shawl.

LAUNDERING INSTRUCTIONS

Every yarn label will have information on how to best care for the finished knitted project.

DYE-LOT NUMBER

Since yarn is dyed in batches, and batches can vary slightly in tone, it is important to use yarn of a single dye lot in a project to prevent color variations. So buy enough to complete your project.

Knitting patterns will tell you how much yarn you will need to complete a project, but if you want to make any changes to the stitch pattern, gauge, or brand of yarn, you will need to adjust the number of balls or hanks that you purchase. To estimate the amount of yarn required to finish a project that you've started, you can measure the square area of what you've already knitted, then divide that measurement by the number of balls of yarn you've used so far. Calculate the finished square area of the total project, then divide this number by the number of balls used up to this point. If all else fails, buy more yarn than you think you'll need. As any knitter will tell you, there's no such thing as too much yarn.

YARN CHOICE AND SUBSTITUTION

Each project in this book was designed for a specific yarn. Different yarns possess their own characteristics, which will affect the way they appear and behave when knitted. To duplicate the projects as seen in the photographs, I suggest that you use the designated yarns.

If you would like to substitute a different yarn, be sure to choose one of similar weight to the one called for in the pattern, keeping in mind that a fluffy mohair will knit up differently than a smooth cotton. Yarn size and weight are usually printed on the label, but for the most accurate test, knit a gauge swatch as follows: Using the needle size suggested on the label, knit a piece of fabric at least 4 in/10 cm square. Bind off, then block the piece, following the instructions on page 44. Once blocked, lay the piece on a flat surface and count the number of stitches horizontally and rows vertically over 4 in/10 cm. If your swatch has 20 stitches over 4 in/10 cm, for example, the yarn is Size 4 or medium weight (commonly known as worsted weight). You could then substitute another yarn of the same weight for that yarn. (For more information on gauge, see page 13.)

KNITTING NEEDLES

NEEDLE SHAPE

Needles are the essential tools for knitting and come in a few different shapes:

STRAIGHT KNITTING NEEDLES: Standard straight knitting needles have a point on one end and a knob on the other end. They come in pairs and are generally used to knit flat pieces of fabric. They are available in several lengths; choose the shortest length that will fit all your stitches.

CIRCULAR KNITTING NEEDLES: These needles consist of two short knitting needle points connected by a flexible cable that can form a circle. Most often, they are used to knit in the round to create projects without seams, like hats and leg warmers. But many knitters, myself included, prefer to use circular needles even when working back and forth in rows on flat pieces. I've found that while knitting, the cable allows me to distribute the stitches and the weight of the fabric so that stress on the body is prevented.

DOUBLE-POINTED KNITTING NEEDLES: These knitting needles are short and straight, with points on both ends. They usually come in sets of four or five needles, and are used for knitting small circular pieces such as mittens, hats, and socks that have too few stitches to be worked on a circular needle.

NEEDLE SIZE

The circumference of knitting needles determines the size of the needles. Larger needles produce larger stitches and will create fabric with fewer stitches per 1 in/2.5 cm than smaller needles, and smaller needles produce smaller, tighter stitches.

Knitting patterns will suggest the appropriate needle size to make the specific project with the recommended yarn. Knitting needles are marked in either U.S. or metric sizes (and sometimes both). A handy conversion table for knitting needle sizes can be found at the Craft Yarn Council website, www.yarnstandards .com. Note that conversions are rounded, so they may not always exactly match the size specified on the needle package. (For example, a 24-in/60.5-cm measurement will use 24-in/ 61-cm length needles.) Since everyone knits a little differently, you might need a different needle size than called for in the pattern to produce the same fabric. Always test your knitting gauge (see page 13) before beginning a project.

GENERAL KNITTING TOOLS

The following tools are useful as you knit:

TAPE MEASURE

This dressmaker's tool is used to take your body measurements and to measure your knitted pieces accurately.

SCISSORS

You'll use small, sharp scissors to cut yarn—snipping ends or creating pom-poms or fringe.

STITCH MARKERS

You will find countless uses for these colorful little circular markers. They just slip on the needle, and knitters use them to separate certain stitches from others or to mark the beginning of a round when working circularly. In a pinch, you can make your own stitch marker by tying a piece of contrasting yarn into a loop.

YARN NEEDLE

You use this type of needle, which has a blunt tip and a large eye, to sew up seams without piercing the individual strands of the yarn.

CABLE NEEDLES

Cable needles are used to hold one set of stitches out of the way while you work another set of stitches. They are available in various shapes and sizes. I prefer to use a straight double-pointed needle to hold my cable stitches. Find the one that works for you.

STITCH HOLDERS

Knitters slip groups of live stitches onto stitch holders to keep them safe and ready to be worked later. For a small number of stitches, a safety pin can serve as a stitch holder; for more stitches, a spare needle or length of scrap yarn can be used.

ROW COUNTER

This tool is handy for keeping track of how many rows you have knitted. Or, you can just jot down a running tally on a sheet of paper. Tech-savvy knitters can also find smartphone apps to help them keep on track.

CROCHET HOOK

Even expert knitters occasionally drop stitches. A crochet hook is very handy for picking up dropped stitches.

SAFETY PINS

These standard household items come in handy as stitch holders, stitch markers, a safe haven for dropped stitches, and more. The coilless kind are especially useful since they don't get caught on knitted fabric.

YARN SWIFT OR BALL WINDER

These devices make it easy to wind yarn hanks into usable balls. In a pinch, you can even use a friend's willing outstretched arms.

KNITTING BAG

You'll want your supplies available as you knit, so find a roomy knitting bag. Choose one that won't be easily pierced by knitting needles, and avoid Velcro closures since they can snag your yarn.

GETTING STARTED

This section discusses all the basic concepts you need to know to begin knitting, from how to hold the needles and yarn to how to make the basic stitches.

SLIPKNOT

Nearly every knitted piece begins with a simple slipknot, which is an adjustable loop that fits a knitting needle of any size. Here's how to do it:

STEP 1: Starting at least 6 in/15 cm from the end of the yarn, wrap the yarn into a loop, and then place the working yarn (the yarn coming from the ball) beneath the loop. *See fig. 1.*

STEP 2: Use your knitting needle tip to scoop up the strand of yarn coming from the ball, and pull it through the center of the loop. *See fig. 2.*

Continued . . .

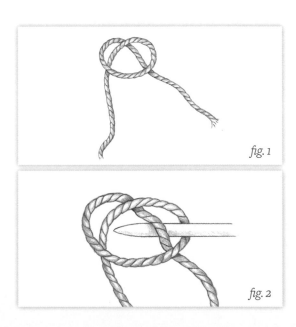

fig. 1

fig. 2

STEP 3: Tighten the slipknot by tugging on both ends of yarn at the same time, adjusting its size to fit the needle while still allowing it to slide easily. *See fig. 3.*

fig. 3

HOLDING THE NEEDLES AND THE YARN

It's been said that there are as many methods of holding knitting needles and yarn as there are people who knit. You may have picked up your style from your grandmother or a friend without even knowing it. Here are the two most common ways. Try both to see which works better for you—it's all about personal preference.

> ### FOR LEFTIES LIVING IN A RIGHT-HANDED WORLD
>
> Most left-handers hold the yarn and needles just like right-handers. Knitting is, after all, a two-handed sport! Just follow knitting directions, substituting "left" for "right," but know there will be some small adjustments you'll have to make in reading more complicated patterns down the road.

ENGLISH STYLE

With this method, the yarn is wrapped or "thrown" around the needle using the right hand. The working ball of yarn is positioned to the knitter's right. *See fig. 4.*

fig. 4

CONTINENTAL STYLE

With this method, the working yarn is held in the left hand, and the right-hand needle is used to "pick" the yarn to create stitches. Many knitters find that the Continental method is faster. And, since there's less movement in this style, some believe it minimizes repetitive stress discomfort. *See fig. 5.*

fig. 5

CABLE CAST ON

Knitters have lots of options for casting initial stitches onto a knitting needle. The "cable cast on" technique is my favorite: it's attractive, quick, and easy to remember.

STEP 1: Begin with a slipknot (page 17) on one needle, and place the needle in your left hand.

STEP 2: Insert the tip of the right-hand needle from front to back into the loop of the slipknot on the left-hand needle, and bring the working yarn between the two needles from back to front.

STEP 3: Use the right-hand needle to scoop up the new loop of yarn you've created and bring it through the old loop toward you.

STEP 4: Place this new stitch onto the left-hand needle.

Congratulations! You've cast on one stitch!

⊛ KNITTING KNOW-HOW

GETTING THE EDGE

If you twist the new stitch while transferring it (by inserting the left-hand needle into the stitch from right to left), you'll create a pretty corded edge. It's the knitter's choice.

CASTING ON MID-ROW

To cast on stitches in the middle of a row, such as when making a buttonhole (see On Neutral Ground, page 115), turn the fabric around, and transfer the left-hand needle to your right hand and the right-hand needle to your left hand. Then use the cable cast-on technique to add the required number of stitches to the needle now in your left hand. Turn the work once more, returning the needles to their original positions, and continue to work across the row.

fig. 1

For each additional stitch to be cast on, insert the tip of the right-hand needle between the first two stitches on the left-hand needle, wrap the yarn between the two needles from back to front, and complete the new stitch as before. *See fig. 1.*

Cast on as many stitches as your pattern requires. If you aren't using a pattern, keep in mind that what looks like 6 in/15 cm on the needle will actually be much wider after you've knitted a few rows. Remember that you can refer to the yarn label to estimate how many stitches you will need per 1 in/2.5 cm.

KNIT STITCH

Believe it or not, knitting consists of just two essential stitches, the knit stitch and the purl stitch. Here's how to make a knit stitch:

STEP 1: Hold the needle with the cast-on stitches in your left hand with the tip pointing to the right. The yarn attached to the ball will be hanging off the right end of the needle; we call this the "working yarn."

STEP 2: With the working yarn in the back, insert the tip of the right-hand needle from front to back into the first stitch on the left-hand needle. *See fig. 1.*

STEP 3: Wrap the yarn around the right-hand needle from right to left, first under and then over the top of the needle. *See fig. 2.*

Continued . . .

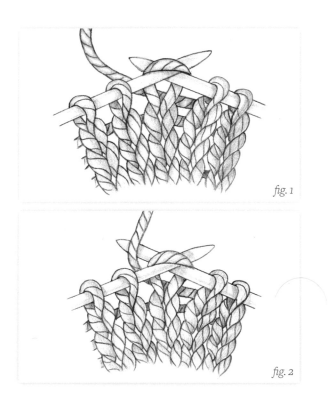

fig. 1

fig. 2

STEP 4: Use the right-hand needle to scoop up the yarn and pull it toward you through the first stitch on the left-hand needle. *See fig. 3.*

STEP 5: Slide the original stitch off the left-hand needle, keeping the new stitch on the right-hand needle. *See fig. 4.*

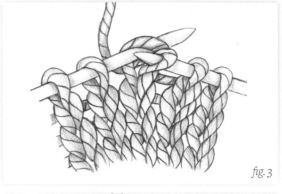

fig. 3

You've just made a knit stitch!

To work a whole row of knit stitches, simply repeat steps 1 through 5 until the left-hand needle is empty. As you knit, make sure that you are wrapping the yarn around the fattest part of the needle; if you work too close to the tip, you'll end up with stitches that are smaller and tight, making them difficult to work in the next row. (Your stitches should fit snugly around the needle but slide easily along the needle.)

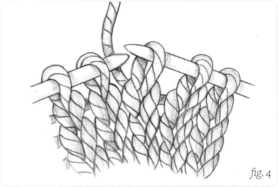

fig. 4

At the end of the row, turn the work by placing the right-hand needle holding all the stitches into your left hand. You're all set to start the next row!

PURL STITCH

The purl stitch is the same as the knit stitch, just made from the opposite side of the fabric. Lots of stitch patterns rely on knit stitches and purl stitches, so you'll want to learn both. Let's make a purl stitch:

STEP 1: With the working yarn in the front, insert the tip of the right-hand needle into the first stitch on the left-hand needle *from back to front* and *from right to left. See fig. 1.*

STEP 2: Wrap the yarn over and then under the right-hand needle, returning to the original position. *See fig. 2.*

STEP 3: Use the right-hand needle to catch the yarn and draw it through the first stitch on the left-hand needle, pushing the right-hand needle from front to back. *See fig. 3.*

STEP 4: Slip the original stitch off the left-hand needle, keeping the new stitch on the right-hand needle. You have just made a purl stitch. *See fig. 4.*

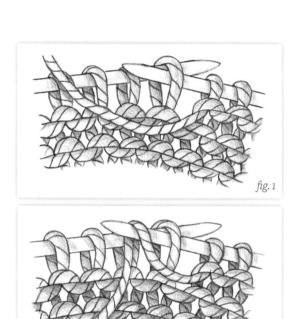

fig. 1

fig. 2

To finish the row of purl stitches, simply repeat steps 1 through 4 until your left-hand needle is empty.

Once the row is complete, turn the work and place the needle with the stitches on it (the right-hand needle) in your left hand. Now you are ready to work the next row!

fig. 3

fig. 4

"KNITWISE" AND "PURLWISE"

Knitting instructions often use the terms "knitwise" and "purlwise" to describe the way that the right-hand needle is inserted into a stitch on the left-hand needle. Knitwise means that you insert the tip of the right-hand needle into the stitch as if you were about to knit that stitch— in other words, with the needle inserted *from front to back, from left to right.* Purlwise means that you insert the tip of your right-hand needle into the stitch as if you were about to purl that stitch— in other words, with the needle inserted *from back to front, from right to left.*

YARN PLACEMENT

When knitting, keep the working yarn to the back; when purling, the working yarn is to the front.

ATTACHING A NEW YARN BALL

When making projects that require more than one ball of yarn (or yarn balls of different colors), you'll need to join a new strand of yarn when one runs out. Here's how: Drop the old color, insert your right-hand needle into the next stitch knitwise or purlwise, depending on what the stitch will be, and, leaving a 6-in/ 15-cm tail, grab the new yarn and use it to make the first stitch. Leave the yarn tails hanging for now (you can tie them in a temporary loose knot if you'd like); you'll weave them in later (see page 48). Your stitches may look loose at this point, but don't worry. When you hide the yarn tails, you'll be able to correct this.

SHAPING

Eventually you'll want to make a project that isn't a rectangle and requires some shaping, like a sweater or mittens. To make your knitting wider, you need more stitches on the needle, and to make it narrower, you need fewer stitches. To accomplish this, you can cast on or bind off stitches. But usually you'll use one of the following techniques to increase or decrease the number of stitches you have.

DECREASES—SINGLE AND DOUBLE

K2TOG DECREASE (KNIT TWO STITCHES TOGETHER)

This single knit decrease eliminates one stitch and slants the stitch toward the right when viewed from the front of the fabric. If a pattern simply says "decrease," this is a good choice.

STEP 1: Holding the working yarn to the back as you do for regular knit stitches, insert the right-hand needle into the first two stitches on the left-hand needle knitwise (see page 25), from front to back and from left to right, as if they were a single stitch.

STEP 2: Wrap the yarn around the right-hand needle as you would to make a knit stitch.

STEP 3: Pull the yarn through both stitches, and slip them off the left-hand needle at once.

You have decreased one stitch.

SSK DECREASE (SLIP, SLIP, KNIT)

This single knit decrease is the perfect mirror image of the k2tog decrease previously described. It slants toward the left, when viewed from the front of the fabric. Both eliminate one stitch, but, if you look closely, you'll be able to see a subtle difference in the way the decreased stitches slant. Designers often pair these two decreases opposite each other to add a decorative effect (as in the sleeve cap shaping in the Get in Line project, page 101).

STEP 1: With the working yarn at the back, insert the right-hand needle from the left to the right into the first stitch on the left-hand needle, knitwise, and slip the stitch to the right-hand needle *without knitting it.*

STEP 2: Slip the next stitch to the right-hand needle in the same way. You have completed the "slip, slip" portion of the decrease.

STEP 3: Insert the point of the left-hand needle into the fronts of both slipped stitches from left to right and knit them together from this position, by wrapping the yarn around the right-hand needle and completing a knit stitch as you normally would.

P2TOG DECREASE (PURL TWO STITCHES TOGETHER)

This single purl decrease eliminates one stitch and slants it toward the right when viewed from the front of the fabric.

STEP 1: With the working yarn in the front, insert the tip of the right-hand needle into the first two stitches on the left-hand needle from right to left, purlwise (see page 25), as if they were a single stitch.

STEP 2: Wrap the yarn around the right-hand needle as you would for a purl stitch.

STEP 3: Pull the yarn through both stitches, then slip both stitches off the left-hand needle at once.

Sometimes you'll want to decrease two stitches at once—a double decrease. To do this, just insert the right-hand needle into *three* stitches at once and either knit or purl them together. These double decreases are abbreviated k3tog and p3tog.

INCREASES

Knitters have lots of choices for increasing the width of a piece of fabric. Here are the most common methods.

YARN-OVER INCREASE

This type of increase is used to create lace and open-work in knitting. The increase creates a little hole or eyelet each time you do it. (The Color Me Mine project on page 79 features yarn-over increases.)

STEP 1: Bring the working yarn to the front, into the purl position, between the tips of the two knitting needles.

Continued . . .

> ### ◈ KNITTING KNOW-HOW
>
> **WORKING INCREASES**
>
> Bar increases are worked *into* stitches, and make-one and yarn-over increases are worked *between* stitches.

STEP 2: As you knit the next stitch, the yarn will go over the right-hand needle to create an extra stitch on the needle.

NOTE: *If the stitch following a yarn over is a purl stitch, you'll need to wrap the working yarn* completely around *the right-hand needle and bring it back to the purl position in the front in order to complete the yarn over. This new stitch will look a little funny on the needle at this point, but when you come to it on the next row, just knit or purl it normally through the front of the stitch to create the eyelet you want.*

M1 INCREASE
(MAKE ONE)

The "make one" increase is made between stitches and uses the horizontal strand of yarn that connects the stitches. The knitter works into the strand, twisting it to prevent a hole. This type of increase is nearly invisible and is often used for sleeve increases. Both knit and purl versions of this increase are possible.

M1 KNITWISE

STEP 1: Use the left-hand needle to scoop up the horizontal strand that's hanging between the needles *from front to back.*

STEP 2: Knit the strand *through its back loop.* This twists the strand to prevent a hole.

M1 PURLWISE

STEP 1: Use the left-hand needle to scoop up the horizontal strand between the needles *from front to back.*

STEP 2: Purl the strand *through its back loop.*

KF&B INCREASE
(A.K.A. BAR INCREASE)

This increase creates two stitches out of a single stitch. The abbreviation stands for "knit into the front and back loops of the stitch."

STEP 1: Insert the right-hand needle into the indicated stitch knitwise (see page 25).

STEP 2: Wrap the working yarn around the needle, as if you were about to knit a stitch, and pull it through *but don't remove the original stitch from the left-hand needle.*

STEP 3: Reinsert your right-hand needle knitwise into the back of the same stitch, and wrap the yarn around the needle to knit a stitch.

STEP 4: Slip the original stitch off the left-hand needle.

ADDING TEXTURE

While all knitting is composed only of two basic stitches, knit and purl, an incredible variety of fabric textures can be created, including ribbing, cables, lace, and more.

GARTER STITCH

This easy-going, noncurling fabric consists solely of knit stitches. Just knit every stitch, every row, and you'll get garter stitch. (Tie One On, on page 71, is knitted entirely of this simple stitch pattern.)

STOCKINETTE STITCH (abbreviated St St)

Stockinette stitch creates probably the most common knitted fabric. For this stitch, you knit on right-side rows and purl on wrong-side rows. The texture of the fabric appears smooth on one side and bumpy on the other. This fabric tends to curl like mad on the edges, so designers often use ribbing to tame the edges.

REVERSE STOCKINETTE STITCH (abbreviated Rev St St)

The back side of stockinette stitch, or reverse stockinette stitch, features the purl side of the fabric.

RIBBING

Fabric comprised of ribbing consists of columns of knit and purl stitches, in which knits are worked into knits and purls are worked into purls. Ribbed fabric is noncurling and elastic, making it perfect for edgings.

Alternating one knit stitch with one purl stitch yields K1P1 ribbing; alternating two knit stitches with two purl stitches yields K2P2 ribbing. Once you get the pattern set up, simply knit the knit stitches as you see them and purl the purl stitches.

Knit and purl stitches can be combined in lots of configurations to create an infinite number of designs—some even look like textured pictures, such as hearts or ladders. Browse a stitch dictionary for ideas. On Neutral Ground (page 115) features a simple but elegant knit/purl fabric.

CABLES

An iconic part of traditional knitting, cables are made whenever one set of stitches changes places with another group of stitches. (The Big Easy, on page 131, shows how dramatic even a single cable panel can be.)

Knitters typically use a cable needle to hold one group of stitches out of the way while another set of stitches is worked. Different patterns can be created, depending on whether the first group of stitches is held in the front or in the back of the fabric, how many stitches are in each group, and whether the stitches are knitted or purled when they are finally worked. Although cables look intricate, they're not difficult to knit, as the following instructions show.

FRONT CROSS CABLE
(A.K.A. LEFT CROSS CABLE)

This example shows a four-stitch cable where two stitches cross in front of two other stitches.

STEP 1: Slip the first set of stitches purlwise (see page 25) onto a cable needle and hold it in front of your work. Make sure the working yarn stays at the back and isn't wrapped around these held stitches.

STEP 2: Keeping the cable needle in front of the work, knit the next group of stitches on the left-hand needle.

STEP 3: Knit the set of stitches that is waiting on the cable needle, making sure that you don't twist them. Put the cable needle aside until it is needed again.

BACK CROSS CABLE
(A.K.A. RIGHT CROSS CABLE)

The back cross cable is almost like the front cross cable, so be sure to re-read those directions for more information. In the example, two stitches cross behind another set of two stitches.

STEP 1: Slip the first set of stitches purlwise (see page 25) onto a cable needle and hold it in back of the work.

STEP 2: With the cable needle in back of the work, knit the next set of stitches on the left-hand needle.

STEP 3: Knit the stitches that are waiting on the cable needle.

Continued . . .

Any number of stitches and combination of knit and purl stitches can be cabled. Two knit stitches can cross over two other knit stitches, for example. Or three knit stitches can cross over two purls. And a front cross next to a back cross makes the staghorn cable (used in The Big Easy on page 131), which looks much more complicated than it is. That's what makes cables so satisfying to knit.

⊛ KNITTING KNOW-HOW

CROSSED CABLES

It can be hard to remember that front crossed cables travel to the left and back crossed cables travel to the right. A trick for keeping them straight is to remember that "front" and "left" both have an F in them.

LACE AND OPENWORK

These delicate-looking stitch patterns use yarn-over stitches (see page 27) to create intentional holes in the fabric. When you are knitting lace or openwork, yarn-over increases are balanced with decreases to keep the stitch count constant (as in Under Wraps on page 179). Just follow the pattern, working increases and decreases as instructed, and the lace will happen like magic!

⊛ KNITTING KNOW-HOW

USING MARKERS BETWEEN REPEATS

Many knitters like to put markers between the stitch repeats when working complex patterns, such as lace, to make following the pattern easier. In most written instructions, asterisks indicate the beginning and the end of pattern repeats.

COLORWORK

Knitters have lots of ways to incorporate color into their work, from simply using gorgeous multicolor yarns to knitting horizontal stripes to working various patterns that employ colorwork. Choosing a combination of colors to use in a project is a way to let your own sense of style shine through. Whether you choose a muted palette or richly saturated tones, you can create something that reflects the personality of the wearer or the spirit of the home.

STRIPES

Basic horizontal stripes are an easy way to play with color in knitting. The only thing you need to know is how to attach a new color. Just use the same method used to join a new ball of yarn (see page 25).

KNITTING KNOW-HOW

MAKING CHANGING COLORS EASY

If you are not working in the round on a circular needle or double-pointed needles, stripes are easiest to work when they consist of an even number of rows for each stripe. This way, instead of cutting the yarn each time, you can simply carry it loosely up the side of the fabric until it is needed again. But if it's not needed for 1 in/2.5 cm or more of knitting, you should probably cut it and reattach it later.

SLIP STITCH PATTERNS

Knitters can use simple slipped stitches to create unique patterns (as in the Boss Tweed, page 137). When a stitch is just transferred from the left-hand needle to the right-hand needle without being worked, it becomes elongated; when a stitch of one color is slipped during a stripe of another color, it gives the appearance of having a second color worked in the row. Now that's what I call easy colorwork!

SLIPPING A STITCH WITH THE YARN IN BACK OF THE WORK (SOMETIMES ABBREVIATED WYIB)

Sometimes you'll be instructed to slip a stitch with the working yarn toward the back of the work. This means you will keep the yarn on the back side of the work (the side away from you) as you transfer the stitch, purlwise (see page 25), from the left-hand needle to the right-hand needle, without working it.

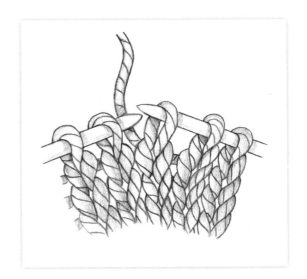

SLIPPING A STITCH WITH THE YARN IN FRONT OF THE WORK (SOMETIMES ABBREVIATED WYIF)

Other times, you'll keep the working yarn toward you, in front of the work, as you slip a stitch. The stitch is slipped purlwise so it is not twisted when you need to work it the next time.

KNITTING IN THE ROUND

Sometimes you'll want to create a tube of knitting fabric, eliminating the need for seams for all or part of a project. (Hats or the Smitten Mittens on page 169 are good examples.) One of the great things about knitting in the round is the time saved at the finishing stage of the project. The right side of the fabric is always facing you as you knit, allowing you to catch any mistakes early—and admire your progress as you go. Depending on the circumference of the knitting, you'll use one of the following methods.

USING A CIRCULAR KNITTING NEEDLE

Cast on the required number of stitches onto the circular needle. Then, take the time to ensure that the cast-on stitches are not twisted by checking that the nubby edge of every stitch is pointing toward the center.

Then, hold the circular needle so that the last cast-on stitch is near the tip of the needle in your right hand and the first cast-on stitch is near the tip of the needle in your left hand. To join the stitches into a circle to begin knitting in the round, knit the first stitch on the left needle, pulling tightly on the yarn to prevent a gap.

USING DOUBLE-POINTED NEEDLES

Since circular knitting needles don't come in short enough lengths to comfortably knit smaller projects such as mittens or the crowns of hats, we use double-pointed knitting needles. It might feel awkward at first holding a handful of needles at once, but you'll get the hang of it quickly.

To start, cast on the required number of stitches onto a circular knitting needle that is the same size (diameter) as the double-pointed needles you'll be using. Move the stitches over to the opposite end of the needle so that you are ready to knit the first stitch you cast on.

For the first round of knitting, knit approximately one-fourth of the stitches from the circular needle onto each double-pointed needle in succession. *See fig. 1.*

Then, form a square out of the four needles, positioning the nubby edge of all the stitches toward the center to make sure the stitches aren't twisted.

With the empty fifth needle, knit the first cast-on stitch, pulling tightly on the yarn to prevent a gap and joining the stitches to begin working in the round. *See fig. 2.*

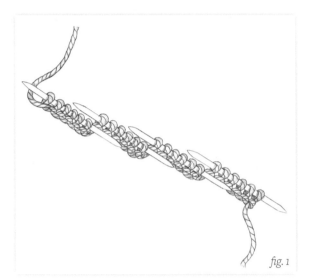

fig. 1

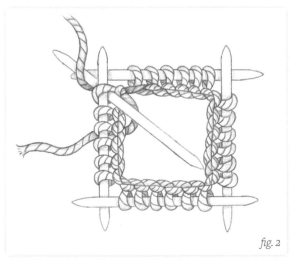

fig. 2

TRACKING YOUR ROUNDS

When knitting on the round, be sure to use a closed-ring stitch marker to keep track of the beginning of the round. Just slip the marker onto the needle between the first and last stitches of the round.

PLACING A STITCH MARKER

When knitting with double-pointed needles, use a closed-ring marker to indicate the beginning of the round. Since the marker will fall off if it is put after the last stitch on a needle, either place it before the first stitch or juggle the stitches around on the four needles so the beginning of the round doesn't hit at the start of a needle.

FINISHING

Most projects aren't complete the minute the knitting is finished. For a perfect finish, use these options.

BINDING OFF

Binding off (sometimes called casting off) is the technique that links all the live stitches together so they don't unravel when they are removed from the knitting needles.

STEP 1: Begin by working the first stitch that you want to bind off in the pattern as established.

STEP 2: Work the next stitch in pattern. There are two stitches on the right-hand needle. *See fig. 1.*

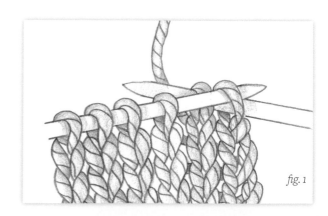

fig. 1

STEP 3: Use the tip of the left needle to lift the first stitch on the right-hand needle over the second stitch and off the right-hand needle. *See fig. 2.*

STEP 4: Repeat steps 2 and 3 for each stitch you want to bind off. *See fig. 3.*

NOTE: *It is important to work in the stitch pattern as established as you bind off. Otherwise, the bind-off edge might be less elastic than the main fabric.*

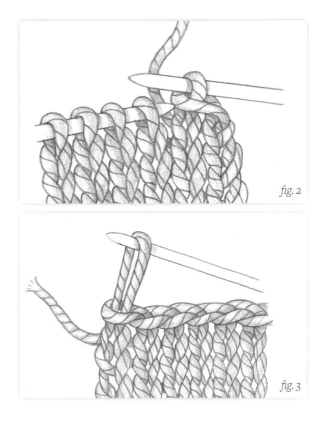

fig. 2

fig. 3

FASTENING OFF

This technique is used to secure that last remaining stitch after all the others are bound off, to end a piece of knitted fabric.

STEP 1: Cut the working yarn, leaving a 6-in/15-cm tail.

STEP 2: Insert the yarn tail into the remaining live stitch, and pull tightly.

PICKING UP AND KNITTING

Some projects require edgings to complete them. The process of picking up stitches from the already knit piece differs, depending on which edge you are working on. When I talk about a horizontal edge, I mean a cast-on or bound-off edge. A vertical edge is the right or left side of a piece, assuming the cast-on edge is at the bottom and the bound-off edge is at the top. Here's how:

PICKING UP STITCHES ALONG A HORIZONTAL EDGE

STEP 1: With the right side facing you, insert a knitting needle *into the middle* of the first stitch just inside the cast-on or bound-off edge. Be sure to go into the center of the V, not into the links of the chain running along the top of the fabric.

STEP 2: Wrap the yarn around the needle as you would to knit and use the tip of the needle to pull up a loop, creating a stitch.

STEP 3: Repeat steps 1 and 2, picking up one stitch in each stitch across.

PICKING UP STITCHES ALONG A VERTICAL EDGE

STEP 1: With the right side facing you, insert a knitting needle *between the first and second stitches* in the first row of knitting. Do not insert the needle in the middle of a V but rather between two stitches.

STEP 2: Wrap the yarn around the needle knitwise, and use the tip of the needle to pull up a loop, creating a stitch.

STEP 3: Repeat steps 1 and 2 to pick up stitches along the edge.

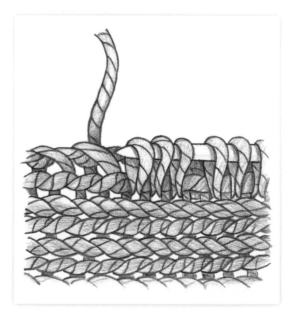

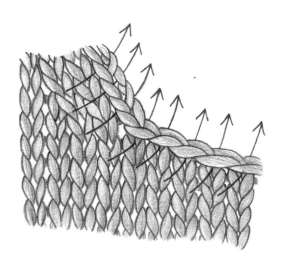

PICKING UP STITCHES ALONG A CURVED EDGE

Along the curved edge of a piece of knitted fabric, such as a neckline, pick up the stitches inside the edge, which will sometimes be more like a horizontal edge and sometimes more like a vertical edge. It's okay to be more than a stitch away from the edge if you need to keep the curve smooth and hide an uneven edge.

PICKING UP LOTS OF STITCHES

Unless otherwise instructed, place the knitted piece so that the right side is facing you. If you're picking up lots of stitches, such as for the border of a blanket, use a circular knitting needle so that all those stitches will fit on the needle.

A GOOD RATIO

Because of the difference in dimensions between the stitch gauge and the row gauge in stockinette stitch fabric, pick up one stitch in each of three rows, *and then skip one row.* If you pick up one stitch in every row of stockinette stitch fabric rather than in three out of every four rows along the edge, the border will ripple. In garter stitch fabric, however, pick up one stitch for every two rows (which is easy, because two rows make one visible ridge) because of the relationship between the stitch and row gauges for garter stitch fabric.

AVOIDING GAPS

Avoid picking up stitches in obvious holes in your fabric, because doing so will actually accentuate the hole, not hide it.

BLOCKING

Blocking is a finishing process that helps "set" your project pieces to the desired size prior to seaming and serves to even out the stitches, almost magically making the overall fabric look perfectly knit.

Knitters have several methods for blocking, but here are two common methods:

WET BLOCKING

Launder the knitted pieces, being sure to follow the manufacturer's instructions on the yarn label. Lay the pieces flat on a padded surface out of direct sunlight, patting them gently to your desired measurements (usually given in a schematic illustration in the pattern). Using rust-proof pins, pin the damp fabric down and allow it to dry.

STEAM BLOCKING

Place a damp cloth over each piece, and carefully run a steam iron just above the fabric. Always check the yarn label first to be sure that it can take the heat. *Never touch a hot iron directly onto your knitted fabric or else you might damage it by flattening it or melting it!*

MATTRESS STITCH SEAMS

Knitters have lots of choices for sewing together their project pieces. I prefer mattress stitch seams, since this technique gives the most invisible result. Typically, use the project knitting yarn to sew the seams; if the yarn is especially brittle or fuzzy, choose a matching seaming yarn that is smooth and even.

VERTICAL MATTRESS STITCH

This method is typically used to sew the side seams of garments or to create a seam anywhere two vertical edges need to be joined.

STEP 1: With the right side of the fabric facing you, lay the fabric pieces flat, side by side. Take care to match stripes, if applicable.

STEP 2: Thread a blunt-end yarn needle with a length of the sewing yarn. (For sewing a seam in most projects, it's best to use the main color yarn used in the project, but for a project knit in a highly textured yarn, you might choose a smooth yarn in the same color.) Beginning at the bottom, bring the needle *from back to front* through the left-hand piece of fabric, one stitch in from the side edge. Be sure to leave a 6-in/15-cm tail.

STEP 3: Bring the needle up *from back to front* through the corresponding spot on the right-hand piece, pulling on the yarn to secure the lower edges together.

STEP 4: Insert the needle down, *from front to back, into the same place on the left-hand piece where the needle emerged before* and bring it up through the corresponding spot in the next row of fabric, grabbing the horizontal bar that is between the stitches.

STEP 5: Move to the piece on the right-hand side and do the same thing: Insert the needle down *from front to back into the same spot on the right-hand piece where the needle emerged before* and bring it up through the corresponding spot in the next row of fabric, grabbing the horizontal bar that is between the stitches.

STEP 6: Repeat steps 4 and 5 several times, grabbing the horizontal bars between the stitches, until you've sewn about 2 in/5 cm. Then pull firmly on the sewing yarn, bringing the pieces of knitting together. Continue this way until the seam is complete, then cut the yarn, leaving a 6-in/15-cm tail. The edge stitches of each piece of fabric will roll to the wrong side. *See fig. 1.*

fig. 1

HORIZONTAL MATTRESS STITCH

This method of seaming is useful for shoulder seams of garments, or any time you're joining bound-off or cast-on edges.

STEP 1: With the right side of the fabric facing you, lay the pieces flat, with their bound-off edges together, placing one piece above the other.

STEP 2: Using a blunt-end yarn needle with the seaming yarn, leave a 6-in/15-cm tail, and bring the needle up *from back to front one-half stitch in* on the right-hand edge of the upper piece of fabric just above the bound-off edge.

STEP 3: Bring the needle down *from front to back* into the center of the corresponding stitch in the lower piece of fabric just below the bound-off edge.

STEP 4: Bring the needle up *from back to front* through the center of the next stitch on the lower piece of fabric.

STEP 5: Return to the upper piece of fabric, and insert the needle down *into the same place it emerged before*, go under a full stitch (both "legs"), and bring the needle up from back to front.

STEP 6: Return to the lower piece of fabric, insert the needle down *into the same place it emerged before*, and bring it up through the center of the next stitch to the left.

STEP 7: Repeat steps 1 through 6 until the seam is completed. On a long seam, pull the sewing yarn gently but firmly about every 2 in/5 cm to close the seam.

Continued . . .

STEP 8: Leaving a 6-in/15-cm tail, cut the yarn. Notice how you're creating V-shaped stitches as you sew, imitating knit stitches. This makes the seam invisible. *See fig. 2.*

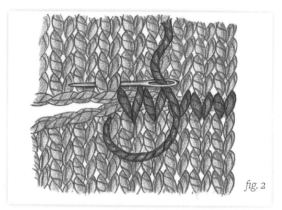

fig. 2

HORIZONTAL-TO-VERTICAL MATTRESS STITCH

This type of seam is useful for setting in the sleeves of garments.

STEP 1: Lay the two pieces of fabric right-side up, with the edges to be joined just touching. The piece closest to you should have the horizontal edge at the top. The upper piece should be oriented with its cast-on and bound-off edges to either side, perpendicular to the bottom piece.

STEP 2: Leaving a 6-in/15-cm tail, and using a blunt-end yarn needle, bring the working yarn up *from back to front* through the center of the first stitch on the bottom piece of fabric.

STEP 3: On the upper piece of fabric, insert the needle *from right to left*, catching the running thread (or bar) that is between the first two stitches at the right-hand edge of the fabric.

STEP 4: Return to the bottom piece, and insert the needle down *into the same spot it emerged before*, then take it up through the center of the next stitch to the left.

STEP 5: Return to the upper piece, and insert the needle down *into the same spot it emerged before*, bringing it up *from right to left* to catch the next running strand (or bar) between the first and second stitches.

STEP 6: Repeat steps 4 and 5 until the seam is completed, then, leaving a 6-in/15-cm tail, cut the yarn. *See fig. 3.*

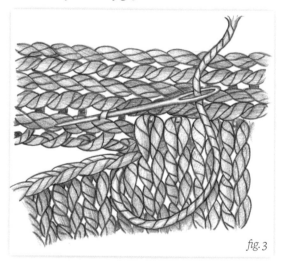

fig. 3

🌀 KNITTING KNOW-HOW

GETTING A GOOD RATIO

Since the stitch gauge and row gauge of stockinette stitch are different, sometimes you'll need to go under two bars on the top piece of fabric instead of one when sewing horizontal-to-vertical mattress stitch seams. The usual ratio is three-to-four: three stitches on a horizontal edge to four rows on a vertical edge. You may want to pin or tack pieces together first so you can ease them together by taking an extra stitch now and then.

HIDING YARN TAILS

When beginning and ending a piece of knitting (and also whenever you attach a new ball of yarn), leave a 6-in/15-cm yarn tail. Once the knitting is completed, you'll darn these yarn ends in on the wrong side of the fabric, securing them so they won't pop out. Here's how:

STEP 1: Use a pointed-tip yarn needle to make short running stitches on the wrong side of the fabric in a diagonal line for about 1 in/2.5 cm, piercing the yarn strands that comprise the stitches to help secure the yarn. Make sure that the stitches don't show on the right side—the public side—of the fabric. *See fig. 1.*

STEP 2: Stitch back to where you began, going alongside your previous running stitches. *See fig. 2.*

STEP 3: To secure the tail, work another stitch or two, this time actually piercing the stitches you just created. *See fig. 3.*

STEP 4: To finish, cut the yarn close to the fabric.

fig. 1

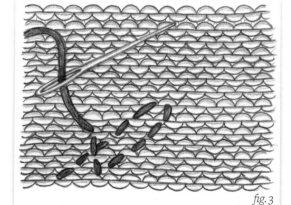

fig. 2

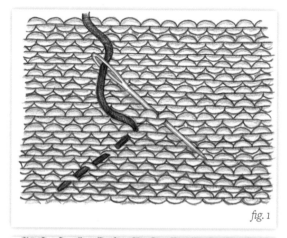

fig. 3

⊛ KNITTING KNOW-HOW

LESS IS MORE

If your knitted project will require seaming, begin and end each piece of fabric with extra long tails. Later you can use these yarn ends to sew your seams. That way, you'll have fewer tails to hide. Bonus!

READING KNITTING PATTERNS

Knitting patterns provide written instructions for creating projects. When you think about it, it's pretty amazing that a designer can write out a couple of pages telling you exactly what tools to use and what movements to make to re-create a garment. But to decipher patterns, you'll need to learn the conventions and "secret code" of those patterns. Read through the entire pattern before getting started so you'll know what to expect. Knitting patterns are usually comprised of several sections. Here's how to interpret them.

SKILL LEVEL

Some patterns include a skill level, which indicates the technical ability level of the project. The projects in this book are in order of difficulty, starting with the simplest project and ending with the most difficult. If you're a beginner, you'll probably want to start with beginner projects, but don't be intimidated by suggested skill level notations. Look over the pattern for unfamiliar abbreviations or techniques and read up on those before beginning. You can always try out the new skills while you're swatching. If you love a knitted project, learn the skills and go for it.

SIZES

This section lists all the sizes that a pattern is written for. Parentheses separate larger sizes from the smaller ones. Babe in the 'Hood, for example, on page 107, is written for multiple sizes. They are indicated like this: Baby size 6 months (12 months, 18 months, 24 months). This means that if you're knitting the 6 months size, you will use the first set of instructions throughout the project; for the 12 months size, you'll use the first set of instructions inside the parentheses; and so on. Garment sizes are based on your actual chest measurement, which is probably not the same as your clothing size or your bra size. Before you begin knitting a garment, take the time to grab a tape measure, take your measurements, and jot them down. Then choose the appropriate size to knit.

FINISHED MEASUREMENTS

Here, you'll find the finished measurements for all sizes of the project that are included in the pattern, such as chest or bust circumference, and length. These numbers reflect the measurements after sewing the seams. If you are having trouble deciding what size to knit even after measuring yourself, measure a ready-made garment of a similar style that fits well and compare these numbers to the finished measurements. This method can work especially well when you are knitting a gift for someone and don't have the opportunity to measure that person without giving away the surprise. Just grab their favorite sweater and measure it!

YARN, NEEDLES, NOTIONS

This section lists all the tools and materials you'll need to complete the project. In this book, I've included the Craft Yarn Council of America's yarn weight information in each pattern so you can easily substitute other yarn if you wish.

GAUGE

Gauge refers to the number of stitches and rows per a specific section of knitted fabric, and it reflects the size of each individual stitch. It is essential to understand how gauge works so you can control the finished size of your knitted projects.

Several factors affect the size of stitches: thick yarns create larger stitches than finer ones; big, fat knitting needles produce larger stitches than smaller ones; metal needles often result in looser stitches than wooden ones. Even your mood can affect your gauge: Nervously knitting during a scary movie might yield a tighter gauge than knitting while lying on the beach on vacation (don't ask me how I know).

Commercial patterns, and those in this book, are written for a particular gauge. For your finished project to be the same size as the one listed in the Finished Measurements section of the pattern and to match the one photographed, you must consistently obtain the gauge called for. So be sure to measure your gauge correctly (and frequently) as you work.

Often, patterns will indicate the desired gauge over 4 in/10 cm rather than over 1 in/2.5 cm. Since individual stitches tend to vary slightly in size, measuring over a larger area yields a more accurate determination of the gauge of the fabric.

SWATCHING

Before you begin a project, knit a gauge swatch in the stitch pattern used for the project, to measure your gauge. Bind off all stitches, and then pin the fabric on a flat surface. Make sure that your piece of knitted fabric is at least 5 in/12.5 cm square, since you don't want to include the edge stitches on all sides of the fabric as you measure. The edge stitches—called selvedge stitches—tend to be uneven in size and are not representative of your fabric. Those stitches will mostly be hidden within the seams of your project and will not affect the finished measurements.

Using a ruler or a specialized gauge measuring gadget laid parallel with a row of knitting, count the number of stitches over 4 in/10 cm, staying away from the edges of the fabric, and being careful not to press down on the fabric which could distort the stitches. It can help to use a pencil or knitting needle to point at the center of each stitch you are counting so you don't lose track. Measure in a couple of places on your fabric to be sure you have the most accurate count. *See fig. 1.*

Divide that number by 4 to establish your stitch gauge (stitches per 1 in/2.5 cm). In our example, there are 20 stitches over 4 in/10 cm, making our gauge 5 stitches to the inch.

If you come up with partial stitches, don't just ignore them! The difference of half of a stitch per 1 in/2.5 cm on a small piece of knitted fabric can be dramatic over a large piece. If you measure 22 stitches over 4 in/10 cm, then your gauge is 5½ stitches per 1 in/2.5 cm. A sweater can end up a full size off—or more—if you are knitting with the wrong gauge.

If, in your gauge, you have fewer stitches per 1 in/2.5 cm than specified in the pattern, then switch to smaller knitting needles. If you have more stitches, then switch to larger needles. Try changing one needle size to see if that makes a difference. Keep changing needle sizes, knitting up swatches, and re-measuring until you obtain the gauge required. *When knitting, it doesn't matter what size knitting needles you use, only that your gauge matches the one called for in the pattern.* It is worth taking the time to obtain the correct gauge at the very beginning. You will ensure that you'll be happy with your finished project. Besides, any time spent knitting is fun, right?

The *row gauge* is often less crucial than the *stitch gauge*, because patterns usually tell you to stop knitting or to add shaping once you reach a

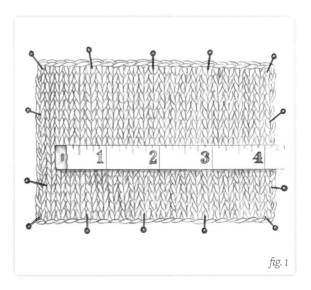

fig. 1

certain measurement instead of after reaching a particular number of rows. But it is still important to check the row gauge, particularly if you are working a stitch or color pattern that depends on completing a certain number of rows before you move on to the next part of the pattern.

Often, you'll find that you get the right stitch gauge, more or less, with needles of two different sizes. To decide which size is best, look at your row gauge. To do so, after blocking your swatch, lay your ruler perpendicular to your rows and parallel with a column of stitches. Count the number of stitches (they will look like Vs if it's stockinette stitch) over 4 in/10 cm and then divide by four. Measure the piece in a few places to come up with an average number. For garter stitch, it's easiest to count "garter ridges," but just remember that each horizontal garter ridge is really two rows.

KNITTING KNOW-HOW

WHAT TO DO WITH A LOOSE GAUGE

Many knitters become more relaxed as they knit a project, and their gauge tends to get looser as they go. If you notice this happening, you can switch to smaller knitting needles to tighten your gauge.

BLOCKING

If you plan to block your project pieces, be sure to block your gauge swatch prior to measuring it. That way you can know what will happen to the knitted fabric when it is laundered. You'll want to knit with that information in mind.

NEEDLES AND GAUGE

Knitting needles are made of various materials, including wood, metal, and plastic. Sometimes different knitting needles *of the same size* will give you different gauges, because the material they're made of can affect the way you knit. Metal needles tend to yield looser stitches because of the way the yarn glides over them; wooden needles often give tighter gauges because the yarn sticks to them slightly. If your gauge is just slightly off from what is called for in a pattern, try switching to another needle of the same size made of another material. Some knitters, for example, prefer smooth metal needles when working with wool or sticky bamboo needles when knitting with slick cottons.

SKILL SET

The patterns in this book provide a section listing the knitting and finishing techniques necessary to make the project. If something looks unfamiliar to you, don't let it stop you! Refer to the pages indicated to learn new skills or to refresh your memory.

PATTERN NOTES

This section of the pattern alerts you to special information that is crucial to the success of your project. For example, you might find specific instructions about assembly or shaping techniques.

STITCH PATTERNS

Each stitch pattern used to create the project is listed in this section. Some stitch patterns require a certain number of stitches in order for them to line up correctly across a knitted row. In those cases, the multiple of stitches necessary will be indicated here. Some patterns will say something like "over a multiple of 5 stitches, plus 2 stitches." This means that the repeated part of the pattern is 5 stitches, but you will need 2 extra stitches at the end to make the pattern symmetric. The correct number is given in the pattern, but to figure out a good number to knit for your gauge swatch, if you want about 20 stitches, you should use 22, because 20 is a multiple of 5 and you need to add 2 more stitches to that to balance the pattern.

PATTERN INSTRUCTIONS

This section gives the instructions for making the pieces of the project: the back, front, sleeves, and so on. Look through the instructions to review the individual sections for each pattern piece. Areas that are crucial to shaping (such as armhole or neckline shaping) of the pattern pieces are set off in separate paragraphs.

Since patterns are written for more than one finished size, in the instructions you'll encounter numbers that you won't need while making one specific size. When making Get in Line on page 101, for example, the sleeve instructions tell you to increase "every other row 0(0, 0,

0, 0, 4) times, every 4 rows 0(0, 2, 8, 17, 18) times, every 6 rows 4(8, 12, 8, 2, 0) times, then every 8 rows 7(4, 0, 0, 0, 0) times." If you're knitting the smallest size sweater, for instance, you would ignore the part about "every other row" and "every 4 rows" because of the zeros. Your first sleeve increase would come on the sixth row of the knitting for this section. Some knitters find it helpful to circle all the numbers in the pattern that pertain to the size they're making. And you might want to make a photocopy of the pattern you're making so you can carry it easily in your knitting bag and make any notes or marks on it you need to.

FINISHING

This section of the pattern details all the steps, in order, required for completing the project, including blocking, seaming, and adding any embellishments such as borders, tassels, and fringe. After spending the effort knitting up your pieces, take your time finishing up these last steps of the project. It will surely be worth the effort.

SCHEMATIC ILLUSTRATION

Many patterns include a schematic illustration, which shows the individual pieces of the project laid flat and provides all important measurements. The drawing comes in handy when deciding which size to knit and when you are blocking the pieces.

ABBREVIATIONS

The terminology in written knitting patterns may appear foreign at first, but you'll soon be accustomed to this shorthand. Long, wordy instructions would take up lots of space on the printed page and can appear even more daunting than the abbreviations. Be patient with yourself as you learn the new vocabulary. Here's a list of standard knitting abbreviations used in this book.

BO — bind off (see page 40)

CC — contrast color

cm — centimeter(s)

cn — cable needle

CO — cast on (see page 20)

g — gram(s)

k — knit (see page 21)

k1p1 — knit one stitch, purl one stitch

k1-tbl — knit one stitch through back loop (see page 73)

k2tog — knit two stitches together in their front loops as one stitch (see page 26)

k3tog — knit three stitches together (see page 27)

kf&b — knit into front and back of stitch (bar increase) (see page 29)

m — meter(s)

M1 knitwise — insert the left-hand needle under the horizontal strand between two stitches from front to back, and knit the picked-up strand *through its back loop* (see page 29)

M1 purlwise — insert the left-hand needle under the horizontal strand between two stitches from front to back, and purl the picked-up strand *through its back loop* (see page 29)

MC — main color

mm — millimeter(s)

oz — ounce(s)

p — purl (see page 24)

p2tog — purl two stitches together (see page 27)

p3tog — purl three stitches together (see page 27)

rev — reverse

Rev St St — reverse stockinette stitch

rnd(s) — round(s)

RS — right side of fabric; the side typically visible during normal use

ssk — slip the first and second stitches *one-at-a-time knitwise* from the left-hand needle to the right-hand needle, then insert the tip of the left-hand needle into the fronts of these stitches and knit them together from this position (page 26)

st(s) — stitch(es)

St St — stockinette stitch

wyib — with yarn in back (see page 36)

wyif — with yarn in front (see page 36)

WS — wrong side of fabric; the side not typically visible during normal use

yd — yard(s)

* or ** — repeat the instructions after the asterisk or between asterisks across the row or for as many times as instructed

( ) — repeat the instructions within the parentheses for as many times as instructed

[ ] — repeat the instructions within the brackets for as many times as instructed

OTHER TERMINOLOGY

As you work through the book, you might come across other wording in instructions that seems unfamiliar. Here's a list of some common knitting expressions.

AT THE SAME TIME

This phrase means that you should work the instructions immediately preceding it with the instruction immediately following it. For instance, if you are doing decreases to shape armholes and need to continue with a stripe pattern, you might see the instruction to decrease every RS row 3(4, 5, 6, 8) more times and, *at the same time*, work 4-row stripes in the following color sequence: A, B, A, C, A, D, A, B. Think of "at the same time" as a warning to slow down and take notice of pattern details before continuing in a pattern. When you see that phrase, read through the whole section before you forge ahead. If the instructions still seem complicated, grab a piece of paper and write down what you'll do on each row, then check them off as you knit.

BIND OFF IN THE PATTERN

To bind off in the pattern, continue working the stitch pattern as established as you are binding off. For instance, if you are knitting a K1P1 Rib Pattern, you would knit 1 stitch, purl 1 stitch, bind off the knit stitch by bringing it over the purl stitch, bring the yarn to the back, knit the next stitch, bring the purl stitch over the knit stitch, and so on. This creates an edge that matches your knitting—while maintaining the relative elasticity of the pattern you are knitting—most closely. If your bind off seems too tight, use a larger needle to bind off the last row.

CHANGE TO LARGER NEEDLES

Often mentioned after a ribbed section is completed, this phrase means you should discontinue working with the smaller size needles

and use the larger ones for the next section of knitting. For the first row of switching to a larger size, simply use one of the larger needles to knit off the smaller needle.

CONTINUE IN PATTERN AS ESTABLISHED

This phrase means you should maintain the stitch pattern as set forth. If you've worked two rows in K1P1 Rib Pattern, continue to knit the knit stitches and purl the purl stitches. This instruction can become a little tricky if you are increasing or decreasing while you are following a stitch pattern. You will want the pattern to continue lining up, even if you've decreased several stitches. The edge stitches can be confusing, though, so you might look a few stitches in from the edge to understand the pattern, and then count back to figure out what to do. You can use stitch markers to mark the borders between larger stitch patterns to help keep you on track.

END AFTER A RS (OR WS) ROW

When instructions say "end after a RS row," the last row worked should be a right-side row. If the pattern tells you to end after a WS row, stop after completing a wrong-side row.

EVERY OTHER ROW

This phrase means you will be alternately working a plain, or even, row with a special kind of row, usually an increase or decrease row. Most often, the right-side row is the "action" row; the wrong-side row is a chance to catch your breath.

EVERY 4 ROWS

Usually used during shaping, this phrase means you will do something on one row and then work three rows without any changes. If the "do-something row" is a right-side row, it will always be a right-side row. You may find that it helps to use a row counter or make tick marks on your copy of the pattern to remember where you are.

FINISHED BUST

This measurement is the circumference of the garment at the chest, just under the arms, after seaming.

FROM THE BEGINNING

Usually used when referring to length measurements, this phrase means you should measure the fabric from the cast-on edge. Some knitting patterns might abbreviate it "from beg."

FRONT (AND BACK) LEG OF A STITCH

Usually, you work a stitch into the front leg to prevent a twisted stitch. And sometimes you will be instructed to intentionally work into the back leg of the stitch to create a special effect. *See fig. 1.*

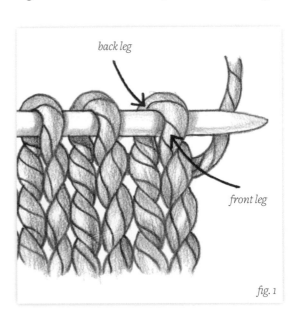

back leg

front leg

fig. 1

FULLY FASHIONED

This term describes a style of shaping. It means that the increases and decreases used to create the tailoring of the sweater are worked away from the edge of the fabric, making them a major element of the garment.

HIDE YARN TAILS

As a necessary part of finishing a knitted piece, you secure the loose yarn ends on the wrong side of the fabric (see page 48).

JOIN

A term used when starting a piece of circular knitting, "join" directs you to connect the first and last stitch of a round to create a circle (see page 37).

JOIN A SECOND BALL OF YARN

Usually used when two sections of a project will be worked simultaneously (such as when shaping two sides of the neckline of a pullover), this phrase instructs you to attach a second ball of yarn to use to complete the row. When working in this way, you do not cut the first ball. Instead, you will knit the left side of the garment with the first ball of yarn, leave it hanging at the neck opening, and then knit the right side with the second ball. On the wrong-side row, you will work the right side with the second ball, leave it hanging, then pick up the first ball, and work the left side. You could work and complete each side of the neck separately, but with this technique, working both sides at once, it will be easier to ensure that both sides of the neck are mirror images of each other.

KNIT THE KNIT STITCHES AND PURL THE PURL STITCHES

Often, the wrong-side rows of pattern stitches are relatively easy rows where stitches are worked according to how they present themselves to you on the knitting needle: if a stitch looks like a knit stitch, you knit it (see page 21); if it looks like a purl, you purl it (see page 24). If you are knitting a rib pattern, the knit stitches will stand forward and the purl stitches will recede.

KNITWISE

If a pattern tells you to insert your needle knitwise, insert your right-hand knitting needle into the indicated stitch *from left to right* as if you're about to knit the stitch (see page 25).

MULTIPLE OF STITCHES

This phrase is used when working textured stitch patterns and indicates that a certain number of stitches must be used. The total number of stitches must be divisible by the number of stitches in the pattern repeat. Occasionally an extra stitch or more is required to balance the pattern.

PICK UP AND KNIT

Used when beginning a border or neckband, this phrase directs you to create stitches along an edge of a piece of already knitted fabric (see page 42).

PLACE MARKER

This phrase directs you to slip a stitch marker on the knitting needle (or sometimes directly onto a stitch, like when knitting the hood in Babe in the 'Hood, page 107) as a guide while working. Often you'll be increasing or decreasing just before or after a marker.

PURLWISE

If a pattern tells you to insert your needle purlwise, insert your right-hand knitting needle into the indicated stitch *from right to left* as if you're about to purl the stitch (see page 25).

SAME AS

This phrase means you will follow the pattern instructions as written for another section of the project up to a specific point. For example, "Work the Front the same as the Back to the beginning of the Armhole shaping," means: Cast on and follow the directions for the Back up to the heading Armhole Shaping, then come back to the directions for the Front for what comes next.

SELVEDGE STITCHES

These stitches are at the very edge of the fabric, and are often different in size and shape from regular stitches. The patterns in this book include the selvedge stitches in the pattern, and they are usually hidden inside the seams.

SEW ON BUTTONS

This part of the pattern usually comes in the finishing stage. Unless you are using a button with very large holes, you will want to choose sewing thread that matches (or perhaps contrasts) with your project. Use a sharp sewing needle to stitch the button in place opposite the buttonhole you created. It's usually best to choose your buttons after you've finished knitting to see which ones fit best in the buttonholes and complement the sweater. A complex project or a vibrant hand-dyed yarn probably deserves understated buttons, but a simple baby sweater like Babe in the 'Hood (page 107) gains a lot of its personality from whimsical buttons, so don't be afraid to experiment.

SLIP STITCHES ONTO A HOLDER

When you see this instruction, transfer the specified stitches from the main knitting needle to a stitch holder by slipping them purlwise, which keeps the stitches untwisted. If you are using scrap yarn as a holder, take a length of smooth contrasting yarn, thread it onto a yarn needle, and run it through the specified stitches while they are still on the knitting needle. When you've got the stitches threaded, take them off the knitting needle, and loosely tie the ends of the scrap yarn together to secure the stitches.

TOTAL LENGTH

This phrase refers to the length measurement of a finished project from the top to the bottom, including the borders.

WITH RS FACING

This phrase means that the piece you are knitting should be oriented so that the right side (or public side) is visible and the wrong side is facing away from you. For example, "You are ready to begin a right-side row."

WITH WS FACING

This phrase means the fabric should be oriented so that the wrong side is visible and the right side is facing away from you. It means that you are ready to begin a wrong-side row.

WORK BUTTONHOLES OPPOSITE MARKERS

This phrase, used in patterns for jackets and cardigans, means you will make buttonholes as instructed so they line up with the button markers on the opposite piece of knitting. Individual knitting patterns usually describe in detail the best method for making the buttonholes for the project.

WORK EVEN

This phrase means to continue knitting and purling in the stitch pattern you've been using without increasing or decreasing stitches.

WORK IN PATTERN AS ESTABLISHED

This phrase means you should continue knitting the stitch pattern (for example, K1P1 Rib) as you have over the preceding rows. The instructions will get you started with the stitch pattern and this phrase simply means "keep doing what you've been doing."

WORKING NEEDLE

This phrase refers to the knitting needle that's being inserted into the stitches on the other needle to create new stitches. For most knitters it is the one held in the right hand.

WORKING YARN

This phrase refers to the yarn you're currently using to create new stitches.

I GOOFED! NOW WHAT?

We all make mistakes as we acquire new knitting skills. Being able to rectify mistakes, such as dropped stitches, simply means learning more knitting skills. So if you encounter a problem, don't panic. Usually you can fix it without having to start over. Here are the most common goofs and how to correct them.

ACCIDENTALLY TWISTED STITCHES

Sometimes you'll notice that a stitch is seated backward on the needle. You can compare a stitch on the needle to a rider sitting on a horse with one leg in the front and one leg in the back: If you look closely though, you can see that the front leg of the stitch is just a bit ahead and the back leg of the stitch is trailing. Sometimes you'll notice that a stitch is seated on the needle with the back leg leading. This is simply an accidentally twisted stitch and it's easy to fix.

To fix a twisted knit stitch, just knit the stitch *through the back of the loop* (the leg of the stitch at the back of the knitting needle). *See fig. 1.*

fig. 1

To fix a twisted purl stitch, just purl the stitch *through the back of the loop* (the leg of the stitch that is at the back of the knitting needle). If this seems awkward, you can turn the stitch around first with your fingers on the needle, and then purl it normally. *See fig. 2.*

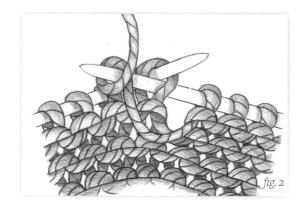

fig. 2

DROPPED STITCHES

Occasionally you accidentally drop a stitch off your knitting needle. Picking it up, even several rows later, is a piece of cake using a crochet hook. Here's how.

For a knit stitch, with the loose strands of yarn *behind* the stitch, insert the crochet hook into the dropped stitch from front to back, then grab and pull through each loose horizontal strand one at a time, starting with the lowest one, until all of the strands are used. Place the stitch onto the left-hand needle, taking care not to twist it. *See fig. 3.*

fig. 3

For a purl stitch, simply turn the fabric around so that the other side is facing you, and pick up the stitch as a knit stitch. A purl stitch is really the back side of a knit stitch, right?

TINKING (unraveling stitches one at a time)

Knitters affectionately call the unknitting of stitches "tinking," since the word "knit" spelled backward is "tink."

To unravel a knit stitch, with the yarn in the back, insert the left-hand needle into the stitch one row below the live one that's on the right-hand needle. Then, slide the tip of the right-hand needle back, allow the loop to drop from the needle, and pull on the working yarn to unravel the stitch. *See fig. 4.*

fig. 4

To unravel a purl stitch, with the working yarn in the front, insert the left-hand needle into the stitch one row below the live one that is on the right-hand needle. Then, slide the tip of the right-hand needle back, allow the loop to drop from the needle, and pull on the working yarn to unravel the stitch. *See fig. 5.*

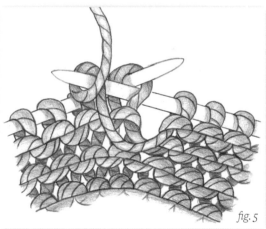

fig. 5

If you need to unravel an entire row (or more), simply remove all the stitches from the knitting needle, and tug gently on the working yarn to unknit each stitch until you've passed the mistake. Use a knitting needle with a smaller circumference to pick up the stitches again. Be sure that the correct "leg" of each stitch is to the front of the needle as you transfer them back to the working needle. You can also just knit them from this temporary needle, using the properly sized needle, if you prefer.

PART 2: PROJECTS

Tie One On

STRIPED TIE

Here's a guy-pleaser that is super easy to knit. It's made using the basic garter stitch, and stripes add just the right amount of pizzazz!

SKILL SET: *Cast on (page 20)* • *Knit stitch (page 21)* • *Knitting a stitch through its back loop (page 73)* • *Attaching a new yarn ball (page 25)* • *Binding off (page 40)* • *Hiding yarn tails (page 48)* • *Blocking (page 44)*

SIZE
One size

FINISHED MEASUREMENTS
Approximately 2 by 60 in/5 by 152 cm

YARN
» Cascade Yarns *Eco Alpaca* (4-medium/
worsted weight; 100% undyed alpaca;
220 yd/201 m per 3½ oz/100 g): 1 hank MC

» Cascade Yarns *Pure Alpaca* (4-medium/
worsted weight; 100% baby alpaca;
220 yd/201 m per 3½ oz/100 g): 1 hank CC

Shown in Silver Twist #1525 [MC] and Midnight
Heather #3025 [CC]

NEEDLES
US 6/4 mm knitting needles (or size needed to
obtain gauge)

NOTIONS
Blunt-end yarn needle

GAUGE
21 stitches and 42 rows per 4 in/10 cm in
Garter Stitch Pattern, blocked

To save time, take time to check gauge.

STRIPE PATTERN
*10 rows of MC, 40 rows of CC;
repeat from the * 5 more times.

**40 rows of MC, 10 rows of CC;
repeat from the ** 5 more times.

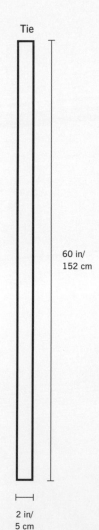

Tie

60 in/
152 cm

2 in/
5 cm

TIE

With MC, use the cable cast-on technique to CO 11 sts.

Row 1 (RS): K1-tbl, k10.

Repeat Row 1 in the Stripe Pattern. The stitch pattern created will be Garter Stitch Pattern. At the end of 600 rows, BO.

FINISHING

Hide the yarn tails.

Block to the finished measurements.

⊛ KNITTING KNOW-HOW

TWIST A STITCH

In this project, you twist the first stitch of every row. The abbreviation k1-tbl means "knit one stitch through the back loop." This creates a neat selvedge edge for the stripe pattern.

CHANGE IT UP!

To knit a scarf for your guy, or even for yourself, cast on 49 stitches and follow the pattern as written.

Taking a Ribbing

COZY RIBBED COWL

This chunky ribbed cowl is made in one piece, with the cast-on and bound-off edges sewn together after the knitting is completed. Since it's knitted out of bulky yarn, you can complete it relatively quickly—and it's super cozy and warm!

SKILL SET: *Cable cast on (page 20)* • *Knit stitch (page 21)* • *Purl stitch (page 24)* • *Binding off (page 40)* • *Hiding yarn tails (page 48)* • *Blocking (page 44)* • *Mattress stitch seam (page 44)*

SIZE
One size

FINISHED MEASUREMENTS
Width: 11 in/27.5 cm

Circumference: 64 in/162.5 cm

YARN
» Plymouth Yarn *DeAire* (6-super bulky
  weight; 100% merino wool; 109 yd/99.5 m per
  3½ oz/100 g): 4 balls

Shown in Philly Fog #401

NEEDLES
US 13/9 mm knitting needles (or size needed to
obtain gauge)

NOTIONS
Blunt-end yarn needle

GAUGE
14 stitches and 12 rows per 4 in/10 cm in the
K2P2 Rib Pattern, blocked

To save time, take time to check gauge.

STITCH PATTERN
K2P2 Rib Pattern (over a multiple of
4 sts + 2 sts):

Row 1 (RS): *K2, p2; repeat from the
* across, ending with k2.

Row 2 (WS): *P2, k2; repeat from the
* across, ending with p2.

Repeat Rows 1 and 2 for the pattern.

COWL

Using the cable cast-on technique, CO 38 sts.

Begin the K2P2 Rib Pattern, and work even until the piece measures approximately 64 in/162.5 cm from the beginning, ending after WS row.

BO in pattern.

FINISHING

Hide yarn tails.

Block to the finished measurements.

Place the cast-on and bound-off edges together. Give one edge a 180-degree turn (a half-twist) and align the edges. Sew the edges together using the horizontal mattress stitch.

◉ KNITTING KNOW-HOW

RIBBING

When knitting the rib pattern, be sure to bring the working yarn between the tips of the needles from the front (for purl stitches) to the back (for knit stitches) and vice versa. Otherwise, you will create yarn overs, which will add stitches and create holes in the fabric.

CHANGE IT UP!

For a traditional rectangular scarf, follow the pattern and just omit the seam.

Color Me Mine

CUDDLY BABY BLANKIE

This sweet baby blanket is knitted on the diagonal. It starts with four stitches, increasing to its widest point, then decreases back down to four stitches. Two rows of eyelets decorate the edges, adding a delicate, elegant touch.

SKILL SET: *Cable cast on (page 20) • Knit stitch (page 21) • K2tog decrease (page 26) • Yarn-over increase (page 27) • Binding off (page 40) • Hiding yarn tails (page 48) • Blocking (page 44)*

SIZE
One size

FINISHED MEASUREMENTS
Approximately 37 by 37 in/94 by 94 cm

YARN
- » Brown Sheep Company *Cotton Fleece* (4-medium/worsted weight; 80% cotton/ 20% merino wool; 215 yd/197 m per 3½ oz/100 g): 5 skeins

Shown in Banana #CW-620

NEEDLES
US 7/4.5 mm circular needle, 29-in/74-cm length (or size needed to obtain gauge)

NOTIONS
Blunt-end yarn needle

GAUGE
20 stitches and 40 rows per 4 in/10 cm in Garter Stitch Pattern, blocked

To save time, take time to check gauge.

PATTERN NOTES
- » This blanket is worked on the diagonal.

- » The circular knitting needle is used in order to accommodate the large number of stitches. Do not join at the end of rows; instead, work back and forth in rows.

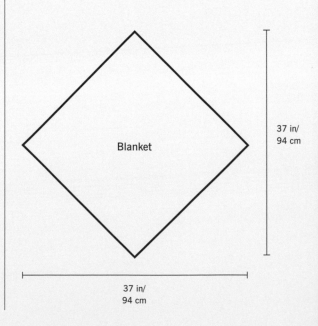

Blanket

37 in/ 94 cm

37 in/ 94 cm

BLANKET

Use the cable cast-on technique to CO 4 sts.

BEGIN INCREASING

Row 1 (RS): K2, yarn over, k2—5 sts.

Row 2: K2, yarn over, k3—6 sts.

Row 3: K2, yarn over, k2tog, yarn over, k2—7 sts.

Row 4: K2, yarn over, k2tog, yarn over, k3—8 sts.

Rows 5–210: K2, yarn over, k2tog, yarn over, knit to the end of the row. Each row will add one stitch—214 sts at the end of Row 210.

BEGIN DECREASING

Row 211 (RS): K1, [k2tog, yarn over] twice, k2tog, knit across 207 sts to the end of the row—213 sts remain.

Rows 212–417: K1, [k2tog, yarn over] twice, k2tog, knit across to end of row. Each row will decrease 1 stitch; there will be 7 stitches remaining at the end of Row 417.

Row 418 (WS): K1, k2tog, yarn over, k2tog, k2—6 sts remain.

Row 418: K1, k2tog, yarn over, k2tog, k1—5 sts.

Row 419: K1, k2tog, k2—4 sts remain.

BO.

FINISHING

Hide yarn tails.

Block to the finished measurements.

⊛ KNITTING KNOW-HOW

GARTER STITCH PATTERN

This pattern is deceptively easy to knit, since you only need to concentrate at the beginning of every row while creating the eyelets. The rest of the row is simply knit stitches. This main fabric is known as Garter Stitch Pattern.

BRACKETS USED IN PATTERNS

Sometimes, brackets are used in knitting patterns to indicate a stitch or maneuver that will be repeated a given number of times, as seen in Row 211. Here's how to decipher that row, word-for-word: K1, k2tog, yarn over, k2tog, yarn over, k2tog, knit across 207 stitches to the end of the row. At the end of the row you'll have 213 stitches remaining.

CHANGE IT UP!

Prefer a smaller project? Knit a snazzy dishcloth! Simply follow the pattern as written until you have 46 stitches total, then begin decreasing as described, and finish as described in the pattern.

Urban Renewal

CHUNKY HAT

Let the yarn do the work! Knitted in simple stockinette stitch in a funky thick-and-thin multicolored yarn, this hat is anything but ho-hum. It's worked in the round from the brim up. Simple decreases form the crown. After knitting this pattern once or twice, it will be easy for you to adjust the number of stitches to create a bigger or smaller hat for someone you love.

SKILL SET: *Using a circular knitting needle (page 37)* • *Cable cast on (page 20)* • *Knit stitch (page 21)* • *M1 knitwise (page 29)* • *K2tog decrease (page 26)* • *Using double-pointed needles (page 38)* • *Hiding yarn tails (page 48)*

SIZE
One size fits most women

FINISHED MEASUREMENTS
Circumference: 20 in/50 cm

Height: 9 in/22.75 cm

YARN
» Knit Collage *Pixie Dust Mini* (5-bulky weight; 99% wool/1% angelina; 80 yd/73 m per 3½ oz/100g): 2 hanks

Shown in Seashell Pink

NEEDLES
US 9/5.5 mm circular needle, 16-in/40.5-cm length

US 10½/6.5 mm circular needle, 16-in/40.5-cm length (or size needed to obtain gauge)

1 set of 5 US 10½/6.5 mm double-pointed needles

NOTIONS
Stitch marker

Blunt-end yarn needle

EXTRAS
Cardboard

GAUGE
11 stitches and 17 rounds per 4 in/10 cm in St St, worked in the round with the larger circular needle

To save time, take time to check gauge.

PATTERN NOTES
» This hat is made from the bottom (brim) up and knit in the round.

» When decreasing for the crown, change from a circular needle to double-pointed needles when there are too few stitches remaining to comfortably knit with the circular needle. Simply work approximately one-quarter of the total number of stitches onto each of four double-pointed needles as you work your way across the round. Use the fifth needle to knit.

STITCH PATTERNS
K1P1 Rib Pattern Worked in the Round (multiple of 2 sts):

All Rnd: *K1, p1; repeat from the * around.

Stockinette Stitch Pattern Worked in the Round (any number of sts):

All Rnd: Knit around.

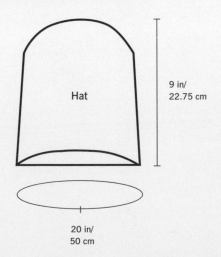

Hat

9 in/ 22.75 cm

20 in/ 50 cm

BRIM

With the smaller circular needle, use the cable cast-on technique to CO 54 sts. Place a marker for the beginning of the round and join, being careful not to twist the sts.

Begin the K1P1 Rib Pattern worked in the round, and work even for 4 rounds. The ribbed brim of the hat is complete.

BODY

Next Rnd (Increase Rnd): *K3, M1 knitwise; repeat from the * around—72 sts.

Change to the larger circular needle, and begin knitting all rounds, working even in St St in the round until the piece measures approximately 7¼ in/18 cm from the beginning.

SHAPE THE CROWN

Rnd 1: *K7, k2tog; repeat from the * around—64 sts.

Rnd 2: *K6, k2tog; repeat from the * around—56 sts.

Rnd 3: *K5, k2tog; repeat from the * around—48 sts.

Rnd 4: *K4, k2tog; repeat from the * around—40 sts.

Rnd 5: *K3, k2tog; repeat from the * around—32 sts.

Rnd 6: *K2, k2tog; repeat from the * around—24 sts.

Rnd 7: *K1, k2tog; repeat from the * around—16 sts.

Rnd 8: *K2tog; repeat from the * around—8 sts.

Do not BO. Cut the yarn, leaving a 12-in/30.5-cm tail.

FINISHING

Thread the yarn tail through a yarn needle, and weave it through the remaining 8 live sts at the top of the hat's crown.

Hide yarn tails except for the tail at the top of the hat. You will use this tail to sew on a pom-pom.

POM-POM

Cut the cardboard into two 4-in/10-cm circles. Cut a ¾-in-/2-cm-diameter hole in middle of each circle.

Cut a ½-in/1.5-cm wedge out of each cardboard circle to create a C shape. This will make it easier to wrap the yarn and cut it later.

Hold the two cardboard pieces together as if one, and wrap the yarn around them many times. More yarn wrapping will create a fatter, more substantial pom-pom.

Take a separate length of yarn about 12 in/30.5 cm long and thread it onto yarn needle. Leaving a 4-in/10-cm tail, run the needle between the two C's of cardboard through all the loops of yarn two or three times before pulling it tight and securing with a knot. Do not cut the yarn tails. You'll use those to sew the pom-pom to the hat. Then slide your scissors between the two pieces of cardboard, and cut through all the strands of yarn around the outer edge of the C shape.

Remove the cardboard from the pom-pom. Fluff up the pom-pom and trim to shape.

Sew the pom-pom into place at top of hat.

Hide the remaining yarn tail.

⊛ KNITTING KNOW-HOW

TEXTURED YARN

Don't be overly concerned about the evenness of your stitches when you knit with a richly textured yarn like this one. Some of your stitches may be larger than others and will add interesting texture to the fabric.

CHANGE IT UP!

For a hat with less slouch, begin the crown decreases when the piece measures 5¾ in/14.5 cm from the beginning.

Pouf Positive

FLOOR PILLOW

Knit this fun pillow to jazz up your home. It is knit in the round using a simple textured knit-and-purl pattern. There's very little shaping: the top and bottom are gathered together by weaving a piece of yarn through the stitches.

SKILL SET: *Using a circular knitting needle (page 37) • Cable cast on (page 20) • Knit stitch (page 21) • Purl stitch (page 24) • Kf&b increase (page 29) • K2tog decrease (page 26) • Hiding yarn tails (page 48)*

SIZE
One size

FINISHED MEASUREMENTS
Approximately 18½ in/47 cm in diameter

YARN
» Rowan *Big Wool* (5-bulky weight;
100% merino wool; 87 yd/80 m per
3½ oz/100 g): 6 balls

Shown in Prize #064

NEEDLES
US 13/9 mm circular needle, 29-in/74-cm length
(or size needed to obtain gauge)

NOTIONS
Stitch marker

Blunt-end yarn needle

Fiberfill stuffing

GAUGE
12 stitches and 16 rows per 4 in/10 cm in the
Spiral Pattern, unblocked

To save time, take time to check gauge.

STITCH PATTERN
Spiral Pattern (over a multiple of 6 sts):

Rnd 1 (RS): *P3, k3; repeat from the *
around.

Rnd 2: Repeat Rnd 1.

Rnds 3 and 4: *K1, p3, k2; repeat from the *
around.

Rnds 5 and 6: *K2, p3, k1; repeat from the *
around.

Rnds 7 and 8: *K3, p3; repeat from the *
around.

Rnds 9 and 10: *P1, k3, p2; repeat from the *
around.

Rnds 11 and 12: *P2, k3, p1; repeat from the *
around.

Repeat Rnds 1 through 12 for the pattern.

POUF PILLOW

Beginning at the bottom of the pillow, and leaving a 20-in/50-cm tail, use the cable cast-on technique to CO 87 sts. Place a marker for the beginning of the round and join, being careful not to twist the sts.

Foundation Rnd (RS): Kf&b into each st around— 174 sts.

Begin the 12-round Spiral Pattern, and work even until the piece measures approximately 18½ in/47 cm from the beginning.

Next Rnd: *K2tog; repeat from the * around— 87 sts remain.

Do not bind off. Cut the yarn, leaving a 20-in/50-cm tail.

FINISHING

Thread the yarn tail onto your yarn needle and bring it through the remaining 87 sts on the needle, remove the knitting needle, and pull the yarn to close up the hole. Then secure the yarn firmly.

Stuff the pillow with fiberfill to desired density.

Thread the yarn tail from cast-on edge onto yarn needle and bring it through the stitches of the Foundation Rnd.

Finish as for bottom.

Hide yarn tails.

KNITTING KNOW-HOW

COUNTING ROWS

Until you become familiar with the stitch pattern, use tick marks or a row counter to keep track of which row of the pattern you are working.

CHANGE IT UP!

Make a smaller version as a toy for Kitty! Simply cast on fewer stitches (but still a multiple of 6) to make a smaller sphere, and add some dried catnip before closing.

Hat Trick

STRIPY BEANIE

Here's a simple project that will please any guy (or gal) on your list. It's the perfect opportunity to practice your ribbing skills! Be sure to move the working yarn between the needle tips to the back before knitting a stitch and again to the front before purling.

SKILL SET: *Using a circular knitting needle (page 37)* • *Cable cast on (page 20)* • *Knit stitch (page 21)* • *Purl stitch (page 24)* • *Attaching a new yarn ball (page 25)* • *K2tog decrease (page 26) and p2tog decrease (page 27)* • *Using double-pointed needles (page 38)* • *Hiding yarn tails (page 48)*

SIZE
One size fits most adults

FINISHED MEASUREMENTS
Circumference: 20 in/50 cm

Height: 8½ in/21.5 cm

YARN
» Cascade Yarns *Greenland* (4-medium/ worsted weight; 100% superwash merino wool; 137 yd/125 m per 3½ oz/100 g): 1 ball MC, and 1 ball CC

Shown in Walnut Heather #3533 [MC] and Ruby #3512 [CC]

NEEDLES
US 8/5 mm circular needle, 16-in/40.5-cm length (or size needed to obtain gauge)

1 set of 5 US 8/5 mm double-pointed needles

NOTIONS
Stitch marker

Blunt-end yarn needle

GAUGE
17 stitches and 22 rounds per 4 in/10 cm in the P3K2 Rib Pattern, worked in the round

To save time, take time to check gauge.

PATTERN NOTES
» This hat is made from the bottom (brim) up in the round.

» When decreasing for the crown, change to double-pointed needles when there are too few stitches remaining to comfortably knit with the circular needle: Simply work approximately one-fourth of the total number of stitches onto each of four double-pointed needles as you work your way across the round. Use the fifth needle to knit.

» There's no need to cut the yarn after each stripe. To save finishing time later, just carry the unused yarn loosely up the wrong side of the hat until it is needed again.

STITCH PATTERN
P3K2 Rib Pattern Worked in the Round (over a multiple of 5 sts):

All Rnds: *P3, k2; repeat from the * around.

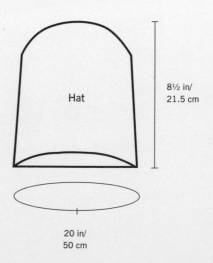

Hat

8½ in/
21.5 cm

20 in/
50 cm

HAT

With the circular needle and CC, use the cable cast-on technique to CO 85 sts. Place a marker for the beginning of the round and join, being careful not to twist the sts.

Set-up Rnds: Work the P3K2 Rib Pattern for 2 rounds.

Rnd 1: Change to MC and knit 1 rnd.

Rnds 2–7: With MC, work 6 rnds of P3K2 Rib Pattern.

Rnd 8: Change to CC and knit 1 rnd.

Rnd 9: With CC, work 1 round of P3K2 Rib Pattern.

Repeat Rnds 1 through 9 once more.

Cut the CC yarn. The remainder of the hat is worked in MC.

Change to MC, and knit 1 rnd.

Work P3K2 Rib Pattern until the piece measures approximately 7¼ in/18 cm from the beginning.

SHAPE CROWN

Rnd 1: *P2tog, p1, k2; repeat from the * around—68 sts.

Rnd 2: *P2, k2; repeat from the * around.

Rnd 3: *P2tog, k2; repeat from the * around—51 sts.

Rnd 4: *P1, k2; repeat from the * around.

Rnd 5: *K2tog, k1; repeat from the * around—34 sts.

Rnd 6: *K2tog; repeat from the * around—17 sts.

Rnd 7: *K2tog; repeat from the * around to the last st, k1—9 sts.

Do not BO. Cut the yarn, leaving a 12-in/30.5-cm tail.

FINISHING

Thread the tail at the top of the hat onto a yarn needle and draw the yarn tail through the 9 sts remaining at the top of the hat; pull gently to close the hole.

Hide yarn tails.

Let It Flow

DRAPEY JACKET

- -

Unstructured and comfortable, this jacket is one you'll turn to often. It is knit side to side in stockinette stitch, so you end up with a contemporary and sophisticated-looking layering piece that's really no harder to knit than a baby blanket. As you knit, you'll create a slit for each armhole. When the body of the sweater is done, you'll make the sleeves using just a few basic increases, and sew them into place. This project is a good choice for knitting a first sweater—and it's sure to get lots of compliments!

SKILL SET: *Cable cast on (page 20)* • *Knit stitch (page 21)* • *Purl stitch (page 24)* • *Binding off (page 40)* • *M1 knitwise (page 29)* • *Hiding yarn tails (page 48)* • *Blocking (page 44)* • *Mattress stitch seams (page 44)*

SIZES

Small(Medium, Large, 1X, 2X). Instructions are for the smallest size, with changes for other sizes noted in parentheses as necessary.

FINISHED MEASUREMENTS

Bust: 34(38, 42, 46, 50) in/
86(96, 107, 117, 127) cm

Length (excluding fold-back collar): 24(24, 25½, 25½, 25½) in/60.5(60.5, 64.75, 64.75, 64.75) cm

YARN

» Malabrigo *Silky Merino* (3-light/DK weight; 51% silk/49% merino wool; 150 yd/137 m per 1¾ oz/50 g): 12(13, 14, 15, 16) hanks

Shown in Camote #404

NEEDLES

US 6/4 mm circular needle, 24-in/61-cm length (or size needed to obtain gauge)

NOTIONS

Blunt-end yarn needle

GAUGE

20 stitches and 31 rows per 4 in/10 cm in St St, blocked

To save time, take time to check gauge.

PATTERN NOTES

» This sweater body is knit in one piece side to side; the sleeves are knit separately.

» A circular knitting needle is used to accommodate the large number of stitches; work back and forth in rows; do not work in the round.

» To ensure random color distribution, work from two different yarn balls, alternating two rows from each.

» The instructions include 1 selvedge stitch on each side for seaming; these stitches are not reflected in the final measurements.

» For fully fashioned increases: K1, M1 knitwise, work in pattern as established across to last stitch, M1 knitwise, k1.

STITCH PATTERN

Stockinette Stitch (over any number of sts):

Row 1 (RS): Knit across.

Row 2: Purl across.

Repeat Rows 1 and 2 for the pattern.

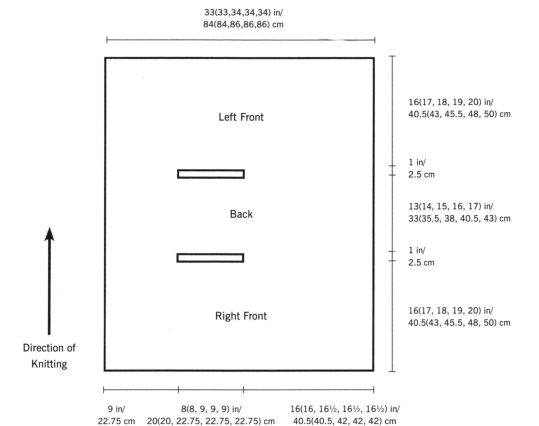

33(33,34,34,34) in/
84(84,86,86,86) cm

Left Front

16(17, 18, 19, 20) in/
40.5(43, 45.5, 48, 50) cm

1 in/
2.5 cm

Back

13(14, 15, 16, 17) in/
33(35.5, 38, 40.5, 43) cm

1 in/
2.5 cm

Right Front

16(17, 18, 19, 20) in/
40.5(43, 45.5, 48, 50) cm

Direction of
Knitting

9 in/
22.75 cm

8(8, 9, 9, 9) in/
20(20, 22.75, 22.75, 22.75) cm

16(16, 16½, 16½, 16½) in/
40.5(40.5, 42, 42, 42) cm

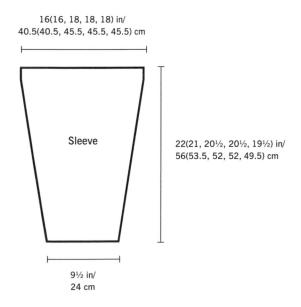

16(16, 18, 18, 18) in/
40.5(40.5, 45.5, 45.5, 45.5) cm

Sleeve

22(21, 20½, 20½, 19½) in/
56(53.5, 52, 52, 49.5) cm

9½ in/
24 cm

Continued...

RIGHT FRONT

Using the cable cast-on technique, *loosely* CO 165(165, 173, 173, 173) sts.

Begin St St, and work even until the piece measures approximately 16(17, 18, 19, 20) in/40.5(43, 45.5, 48, 50) cm from the beginning, ending after WS row.

SHAPE RIGHT ARMHOLE

Next Row (RS): Knit 80(80, 83, 83, 83) sts, BO the next 40(40, 45, 45, 45) sts, knit remaining 45 sts.

Work 7 more rows on these 45 sts only. You will end after a WS row.

Cut the yarn, and reattach it to the remaining 80(80, 83, 83, 83) sts at the armhole edge. Begin with a WS row, work 8 rows, then CO 40(40, 45, 45, 45) sts above the bound-off armhole edge, and work the last 45 sts to the end of the row—165(165, 173, 173, 173) sts.

BACK

Work even on 165(165, 173, 173, 173) sts for another 13(14, 15, 16, 17) in/33(35.5, 38, 40.5, 43) cm, ending after a WS row.

SHAPE LEFT ARMHOLE

Next Row (RS): Knit 80(80, 83, 83, 83) sts, BO the next 40(40, 45, 45, 45) sts, knit remaining 45 sts.

Working only on these 45 sts, work even for 7 rows.

Cut yarn, leaving a tail, and reattach the yarn to the remaining 80(80, 83, 83, 83) sts at armhole edge. Begin with a WS row, work 8 rows even, then CO 40(40, 45, 45, 45) sts above the bound-off armhole edge, and work across the last 45 sts to end the row—165(165, 173, 173, 173) sts.

LEFT FRONT

Continue even until the piece measures approximately 16(17, 18, 19, 20) in/40.5(43, 45.5, 48, 50) cm from the end of the left armhole, or the same as the Right Front, ending after WS row.

BO *loosely*.

SLEEVES (MAKE 2)

CO 48 sts.

Work back and forth in St St, and work fully fashioned increases (see Pattern Notes) every 6 rows 0(0, 13, 13, 17) times, then every 8 rows 4(8, 9, 9, 5) times, then every 10 rows 13(9, 0, 0, 0) times—82(82, 92, 92, 92) sts.

Continue even until the piece measures approximately 22(21, 20½, 20½, 19½) in/56(53.5, 52, 52, 49.5) cm from the beginning, ending after a WS row.

BO.

FINISHING

Hide yarn tails.

Block to the finished measurements.

Sew in sleeves, placing the sleeve seams at the bottom of the armholes.

Sew sleeve seams.

KNITTING WITH A LOOSE GAUGE

This design is intentionally knit using a loose gauge to give the fabric special drape. Be sure to block the pieces to their finished measurements to achieve the desired effect.

CHANGE IT UP!

For a great-looking unconstructed sleeve-less topper, simply omit the sleeves. If desired, pick up stitches all around the armholes, and work 4 rows of garter stitch to finish off each edge.

Get in Line

SPORTY PULLOVER

With its carefully matched-up stripes, this design will soon become a weekend favorite. Be sure to match the row gauge specified in the pattern to achieve the most figure-flattering effect. Hand-dyed yarn makes this project extra-special!

SKILL SET: *Cable cast on (page 20)* • *Knit stitch (page 21)* • *Purl stitch (page 24)* • *Attaching a new yarn ball (page 25)* • *K2tog decrease (page 26), p2tog decrease (page 27), and ssk decrease (page 26)* • *M1 knitwise (page 29)* • *Binding off (page 40)* • *Hiding yarn tails (page 48)* • *Blocking (page 44)* • *Mattress stitch seams (page 44)* • *Picking up and knitting (page 42)*

SIZES

Women's Small(Medium, Large, 1X, 2X, 3X). Instructions are for the smallest size, with changes for other sizes noted in parentheses as necessary.

FINISHED MEASUREMENTS

Bust: 32(36, 40, 44, 48, 52) in/81(91, 100, 112, 121, 132) cm

Waist: 29(33, 37, 41, 45, 49) in/74(84, 94, 104, 114, 124) cm

Hip: 32(36, 40, 44, 48, 52) in/81(91, 100, 112, 121, 132) cm

Length: 20(20½, 21, 21½, 21½, 22) in/50(52, 53, 54.5, 54.5, 56) cm

YARN

» Miss Babs *Yummy Sock Yarn 3-Ply* (2-fine/sport weight; 100% superwash wool; 335 yd/306 m per 5.2 oz/147.5 g: 3(3, 4, 4, 5, 5) hanks MC; 1(1, 1, 1, 2, 2) hanks CC

Shown in Starling Shadows [MC] and Spring Lettuce [CC]

NEEDLES

US 3/3.25 mm knitting needles

US 5/3.75 mm knitting needles (or size needed to obtain gauge)

NOTIONS

Blunt-end yarn needle

GAUGE

24 stitches and 32 rows per 4 in/10 cm in St St, unblocked, with the larger needles

21 stitches and 32 rows per 4 in/10 cm in St St, blocked, with the larger needles

To save time, take time to check gauge.

PATTERN NOTES

» This sweater is knit in four pieces from the bottom up.

» To ensure random color distribution, work from two different balls of yarn of each color, alternating two rows from each.

» The instructions include one selvedge stitch each side for seaming; these stitches are not reflected in the final measurements.

» For fully fashioned decreases: On RS rows, K1, ssk, work across to last 3 sts, k2tog, k1; on WS rows, p1, p2tog, purl across to last 3 sts, p2tog, p1.

» For fully fashioned increases: K1, M1 knitwise, knit across to last stitch, M1 knitwise, k1.

STITCH PATTERNS

K1P1 Rib Pattern (over a multiple of 2 sts):

Row 1 (RS): *K1, p1; repeat from the * across.

Pattern Row: As Row 1.

Stockinette Stitch (over any number of sts):

Row 1 (RS): Knit across.

Row 2: Purl across.

Repeat Rows 1 and 2 for the pattern.

Stripe Pattern:

*2 rows of CC, 6 rows of MC; repeat from the * 9 more times, ending with 2 rows of CC and 2 rows of MC.

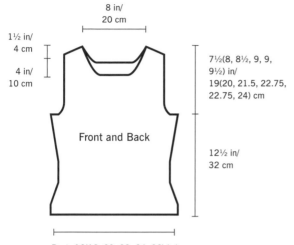

8 in/
20 cm

1½ in/
4 cm

4 in/
10 cm

7½(8, 8½, 9, 9, 9½) in/
19(20, 21.5, 22.75, 22.75, 24) cm

Front and Back

12½ in/
32 cm

Bust: 16(18, 20, 22, 24, 26) in/
40.5(45.5, 50, 56, 60.5, 66) cm

Waist: 14½(16½, 18½, 20½, 22½, 24½) in/
37(42, 47, 52, 57, 62) cm

Hip: 16(18, 20, 22, 24, 26) in/
40.5(45.5, 50, 56, 60.5, 66) cm

13(13½, 14, 15, 16, 18) in/
33(34, 35.5, 38, 40.5, 45.5) cm

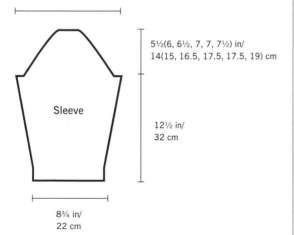

5½(6, 6½, 7, 7, 7½) in/
14(15, 16.5, 17.5, 17.5, 19) cm

Sleeve

12½ in/
32 cm

8¾ in/
22 cm

BACK

With the smaller needles and MC, use the cable cast-on technique to CO 86(96, 108, 118, 128, 138) sts.

Begin the K1P1 Rib Pattern, and work even until the piece measures approximately 1½ in/4 cm from the beginning, ending after WS row.

BEGIN THE BODY AND DECREASE FOR WAIST

Next Row (RS): Change to the larger needles, begin St St in the Stripe Pattern, and, *at the same time,* on RS rows, work fully fashioned decreases (see Pattern Notes) every 6 rows twice, then every 4 rows twice—78(88, 100, 110, 120, 130) sts remain.

Continue even until the piece measures approximately 6½ in/16.5 cm from the beginning, ending after WS row.

INCREASE FOR BUST

Continue the Stripe Pattern as established, and work fully fashioned increases (see Pattern Notes) every 8 rows 0(2, 2, 4, 4, 4) times, then every 10 rows 4(2, 2, 0, 0, 0) times—86(96, 108, 118, 128, 138) sts.

Continue with MC only once the 84 rows of the Stripe Pattern are completed, and work even as established until the piece measures approximately 12½ in/32 cm from the beginning, ending after WS row.

SHAPE ARMHOLES

BO 2(2, 3, 3, 4, 5) sts at the beginning of the next 2 rows, BO 2(2, 3, 3, 3, 4) sts at the beginning of the next 2 rows, then work fully fashioned decreases (see Pattern Notes) every row 0(0, 0, 2, 2, 2) times, every other row 0(3, 3, 6, 10, 11) times, then every 4 rows 2(2, 3, 2, 0, 0) times—74(78, 84, 86, 90, 94) sts remain.

Continue even in the patterns as established until the piece measures approximately 19½(20, 20½, 21, 21, 21½) in/49.5(50, 52, 53.5, 53.5, 54.5) cm, ending after WS row.

Continued…

SHAPE NECK

Next Row (RS): K17(19, 22, 23, 25, 27) sts, join a second ball of MC, and BO the middle 40 sts, knit to end of row.

As you continue, you will work both sides of the neck at once with separate balls of yarn.

Next Row (WS): Purl to the neck opening, drop this strand of yarn; pick up the second strand of yarn, and purl to the end of the row.

Next Row (RS): Knit to the last 3 sts on the first side, k2tog, k1, drop yarn; on second side, k1, k2tog, knit to end of row—16(18, 21, 22, 24, 26) sts remain each side.

Continue even until the piece measures approximately 20(20½, 21, 21½, 21½, 22) in/51(52, 53.5, 54.5, 54.5, 56) cm from the beginning, ending after WS row.

SHAPE SHOULDERS

Next Row (RS): BO 4(5, 5, 6, 6, 7) sts, knit to end; with the second ball of yarn, knit across to end the row.

Next Row (WS): BO 4(5, 5, 6, 6, 7) sts, purl to end; with the second ball of yarn, purl across to end the row.

Repeat these 2 rows twice more.

Next Row: BO 4(3, 6, 4, 6, 5) sts, knit to end, with the second ball of yarn, knit across to end the row.

Next Row: BO 4(3, 6, 4, 6, 5) sts, purl to end; with the second ball of yarn, purl across to end the row.

FRONT

Work the front the same as the back until the piece measures approximately 15½(16, 16½, 17, 17, 17½) in/39.5(40.5, 42, 43, 43, 44.5) cm from the beginning, ending after WS row. Armhole shaping will be complete and you will have 74(78, 84, 86, 90, 94) sts remaining.

SHAPE NECK

Next Row (RS): Work pattern as established across the first 28(30, 33, 34, 36, 38) sts, join a second ball of MC, BO the middle 18 sts, then work to end the row.

Work both sides at once with separate balls of yarn.

Next Row (WS): Purl to neck edge; with the second ball of yarn, BO 5, purl across to end of row.

Next Row (RS): Knit to neck edge; with the second ball of yarn, BO 5, knit across to end of row.

Next Row: Purl to neck edge; with the second ball of yarn, BO 3, purl across to end of row.

Next Row: Knit to neck edge; with the second ball of yarn, BO3, knit across to end of row.

Next Row: Purl to neck edge; with the second ball of yarn, BO 2, purl across to end of row.

Next Row: Knit to neck edge; with the second ball of yarn, BO2, knit across to end of row.

Next Row: Purl.

Next Row: Knit to last 3 sts, k2tog, k1; with the second ball of yarn, k1, k2tog, knit across to end of row.

Repeat the last 2 rows once more—16(18, 21, 22, 24, 26) sts remain each side.

Continue even until the piece measures the same as the back to the beginning of the shoulders, ending after WS row.

SHAPE SHOULDERS

Same as for the back.

SLEEVES (MAKE 2)

With the smaller needles and MC, CO 48 sts.

Begin the K1P1 Rib Pattern, and work even until the piece measures approximately 1½ in/4 cm from the beginning, ending after WS row.

Next Row (RS): Change to the larger needles, begin St St in the Stripe Pattern, and work fully fashioned increases (see Pattern Notes) every other row 0(0, 0, 0, 0, 4) times, every 4 rows 0(0, 2, 8, 17, 18) times, every 6 rows 4(8, 12, 8, 2, 0) times, then every 8 rows 7(4, 0, 0, 0, 0) times, working in MC once the 84 rows of the Stripe Pattern are completed—70(72, 76, 80, 86, 92) sts.

Continue even until the piece measures approximately 12½ in/32 cm from the beginning, ending after WS row.

SHAPE SLEEVE CAP

BO 2(2, 3, 3, 4, 5) sts at the beginning of the next 2 rows, then work fully fashioned decreases (see Pattern Notes) each side every other row 16(19, 22, 24, 22, 24) times, then every row 5(3, 1, 1, 5, 5) times—24 sts remain.

BO 2 sts at the beginning of the next 4 rows.

BO remaining 16 sts.

FINISHING

Hide yarn tails.

Block to the finished measurements.

Use mattress stitch to sew the right shoulder seam.

NECKBAND

With RS facing, using smaller needles and MC, pick up and knit 148 sts along neckline beginning and ending at the open left shoulder.

Work K1P1 Rib Pattern until the neckband measures approximately 1 in/2.5 cm from the beginning.

BO *loosely* in pattern.

Use mattress stitch to sew the left shoulder seam, including the side of the neckband.

Sew in the sleeves.

Sew the side and sleeve seams.

Hide yarn tails.

⊛ KNITTING KNOW-HOW

CHANGING COLORS IN STRIPES

To make your finishing easier (not to mention faster!), don't cut the yarn after each stripe. Instead, carry the yarn loosely up the side of the fabric (see page 35 for instructions).

CHANGE IT UP!

Use your scrap yarns to make each stripe a different color. You'll knit a vibrant, casual sweater and use up your stash at the same time! That's what I call a win-win.

Babe in the 'Hood

BABY'S HOODED JACKET

Knit this little sweater to be the star of the next baby shower! Worked in seed stitch in a heavenly soft cotton yarn, it's sure to be a favorite. Don't let the buttonholes frighten you—they're not difficult. Just bind off a few stitches on one row and cast on a few to replace them on the next row!

SKILL SET: *Cable cast on (page 20)* • *Knit stitch (page 21)* • *Purl stitch (page 24)* • *Binding off (page 40)* • *M1 knitwise (page 29) and kf&b increase (page 29)* • *Ssk decrease (page 26), k2tog decrease (page 26), and p2tog decrease (page 27)* • *Hiding yarn tails (page 48)* • *Blocking (page 44)* • *Mattress stitch seams (page 44)* • *Picking up and knitting (page 42)*

SIZES

Baby's 6 months(12 months, 18 months, 24 months). Instructions are for the smallest size, with changes for other sizes noted in parentheses as necessary.

FINISHED MEASUREMENTS

Chest: 21½(24, 26½, 28) in/54.5(60.5, 67, 71) cm

Length: 11(12, 13, 14) in/27.5(30.5, 33, 35.5) cm

YARN

» Classic Elite *Sprout* (5-bulky weight; 100% organic cotton; 109 yd/99.5 m per 3½ oz/ 100 g): 3(3, 4, 4) hanks

Shown in Summer Rain #4375

NEEDLES

US 9/5.5 mm knitting needles (or size needed to obtain gauge)

NOTIONS

3 stitch markers

Blunt-end yarn needle

Sharp sewing needle

Matching sewing thread

6 buttons, ⅞-in/22-mm diameter (shown with JHB International's Dreamweaver buttons #17632 Yellow and #17633 Robins Egg Blue)

GAUGE

13 stitches and 24 rows per 4 in/10 cm in Seed Stitch Pattern, blocked

To save time, take time to check gauge.

PATTERN NOTES

» This sweater is knit in four pieces from the bottom up; the hood is picked up and worked later.

» Since seed stitch looks the same on the right side and the wrong side, you may want to place a marker on one side or a contrasting bit of yarn to help you keep track, especially when you are shaping the armhole and neck on the front pieces.

STITCH PATTERN

Seed Stitch Pattern (over a multiple of 2 sts + 1 sts):

Row 1 (RS): *K1, p1; repeat from the * across, ending the row with k1.

Row 2: Repeat Row 1.

Repeat Rows 1 and 2 for the pattern.

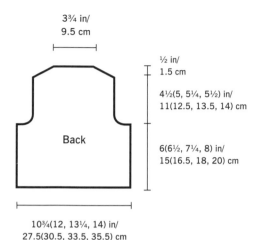

3¾ in/
9.5 cm

½ in/
1.5 cm

4½(5, 5¼, 5½) in/
11(12.5, 13.5, 14) cm

Back

6(6½, 7¼, 8) in/
15(16.5, 18, 20) cm

10¾(12, 13¼, 14) in/
27.5(30.5, 33.5, 35.5) cm

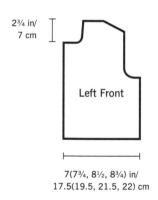

2¾ in/
7 cm

Left Front

7(7¾, 8½, 8¾) in/
17.5(19.5, 21.5, 22) cm

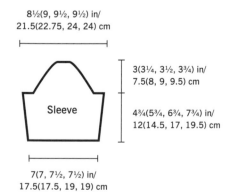

8½(9, 9½, 9½) in/
21.5(22.75, 24, 24) cm

3(3¼, 3½, 3¾) in/
7.5(8, 9, 9.5) cm

Sleeve

4¾(5¾, 6¾, 7¾) in/
12(14.5, 17, 19.5) cm

7(7, 7½, 7½) in/
17.5(17.5, 19, 19) cm

BACK

Using the cable cast-on technique, CO 37(41, 45, 47) sts.

Begin the Seed Stitch Pattern, and work even until the piece measures approximately 6(6½, 7¼, 8) in/ 15(16.5, 18, 20) cm from the beginning, ending after WS row.

SHAPE ARMHOLES

BO 2(2, 3, 3) sts at the beginning of the next 2 rows.

Next Row (Decrease Row): K1, k2tog, work pattern as established across to last 3 sts, k2tog, k1.

Repeat the Decrease Row every row 1(2, 2, 1) more times, then every RS row 2(2, 2, 3) times, working even on the WS rows in between—25(27, 29, 31) sts remain.

Continue even in the pattern as established until the piece measures approximately 10½(11½, 12½, 13½) in/ 26.5(29, 32, 34) cm from the beginning, ending after WS row.

SHAPE SHOULDERS

BO 3(4, 4, 5) sts at the beginning of the next 2 rows, then BO 3(3, 4, 4) sts at the beginning of the next 2 rows—13 sts remain.

BO in the pattern.

LEFT FRONT

CO 25(27, 29, 31) sts.

Begin the Seed Stitch Pattern, and work even until the piece measures approximately 6(6½, 7¼, 8) in/ 15(16.5, 18, 20) cm from the beginning, ending after WS row.

Continued…

SHAPE ARMHOLE

Next Row (RS): BO 2(2, 3, 3) sts, then work in pattern to end of row.

Next Row (WS Decrease Row): Work in pattern to last 3 sts, k2tog, k1.

Next Row (RS Decrease Row): K1, k2tog, work in pattern to end of row.

For sizes 12 and 18 months:
Next Row: Repeat the WS Decrease Row once more.

For sizes 6 and 24 months:
Next Row: Work this row even.

For all sizes: Repeat the RS Decrease Row 2(2, 2, 3) times. Work the WS rows in between even in pattern—19(20, 21, 23) sts remain.

Continue even in the pattern as established until the piece measures approximately 8¼(9¼, 10¼, 11¼) in/ 21(23.5, 26, 28.5) cm from the beginning, ending after a RS row.

SHAPE NECK

BO 8(8, 8, 9) sts at the beginning of the next row (a wrong-side row).

Work 1 row even.

BO 2 sts at the neck at the beginning of the next 2 WS rows.

Use the k2tog technique to decrease 1 st at neck edge once—6(7, 8, 9) sts remain.

Continue even until the piece measures the same as the back to the shoulders, ending after a WS row.

SHAPE SHOULDER

Next Row (RS): BO 3(4, 4, 5) sts, work in the pattern across.

Next Row: Work in the pattern.

Next Row: BO remaining 3(3, 4, 4) sts.

SET UP FOR BUTTONS

Place 3 markers to indicate buttonhole rows. The first should be approximately 1 in/2.5 cm from the top of the neck. Allow 2 to 3 in/5 to 7.5 cm between buttonhole rows, depending on garment size and personal preference (use photo as guide).

RIGHT FRONT

Note that you will be working the buttonholes as you knit the right front. Be sure to read this entire section before you begin.

CO 25(27, 29, 31) sts.

Begin Seed Stitch Pattern, and work even until piece measures approximately 6(6½, 7¼, 8) in/15(16.5, 18, 20) cm from the beginning, ending after RS row.

At the same time, make buttonholes on RS rows opposite the markers as follows: Work 2 sts in pattern, BO 2 sts, work pattern as established across the next 7 sts, BO 2 sts, work in pattern across to end of row.

On the next row, use the cable cast-on technique to CO 2 sts over each set of bound-off sts.

SHAPE ARMHOLE

Next Row (WS): BO 2(2, 3, 3) sts at the beginning of the next row.

Next Row (RS Decrease Row): Work in pattern to last 3 sts, k2tog, k1.

Next Row (WS Decrease Row): K1, k2tog, work in pattern to end of row.

Continued...

For sizes 12 and 18 months:
Next Row: Repeat the RS Decrease Row once more.

For sizes 6 and 24 months:
Next Row: Work this row even.

For all sizes: Repeat the RS Decrease Row 2(2, 2, 3) times. Work the WS rows in between even in pattern—19(20, 21, 23) sts remain.

Continue even in the pattern as established until the piece measures approximately 8¼(9¼, 10¼, 11¼) in/ 21(23.5, 26, 28.5) cm from the beginning, ending after a WS row.

SHAPE NECK

Next Row (RS): BO 8(8, 8, 9) sts at the beginning of the row, then work to the end.

Next Row and all following WS Rows for Neck Shaping: Work even in pattern.

BO 2 sts at the neck edge at the beginning of the next 2 RS rows.

Next RS Row: K1, k2tog, work in pattern to the end—6(7, 8, 9) sts remain.

Continue even until the piece measures the same as the back to the shoulders, ending after a RS row.

SHAPE SHOULDER

Next Row (WS): BO 3(4, 4, 5) sts, work in pattern across.

Next Row: Work in pattern.

Next Row: BO remaining 3(3, 4, 4) sts.

SLEEVES (MAKE 2)

CO 25(25, 27, 27) sts.

Begin the Seed Stitch Pattern.

Use the kf&b technique to increase at the beginning and end of the row every 8 rows 0(1, 0, 0) times, then every 10 rows 2(2, 3, 3) times—29(31, 33, 33) sts.

Continue even until the piece measures approximately 4¾(5¾, 6¾, 7¾) in/12(14.5, 17, 19.5) cm from the beginning, ending after WS row.

SHAPE SLEEVE CAP

BO 2(2, 3, 3) sts at the beginning of the next 2 rows.

Use the k2tog technique to decrease at the beginning and end of the row every 4 rows 0(0, 0, 1) time, every other row 5(6, 7, 6) times, then every row 1(1, 0, 0) time—13 sts remain.

BO 2 sts at the beginning of the next 4 rows.

BO remaining 5 sts.

FINISHING

Hide yarn tails.

Block to the finished measurements.

Use mattress stitch to sew the shoulder seams.

HOOD

With RS facing, beginning and ending 3½ in/9 cm in from front neck edge, pick up and knit 39 sts along neckline.

Row 1 (WS): *K1, p1; repeat from the * across, ending the row with k1. Place a marker on the middle st.

Row 2 (Increase Row): Work in Seed Stitch Pattern as established to 1 st before the marked st, kf&b, k the marked st, kf&b, work the pattern as established across to end of row—41 sts.

Rows 3–5: Work 3 rows even in the pattern, keeping the center st as knit on the RS and purl on the WS and incorporating the increased sts into the pattern established.

Repeat the last 4 rows 4 more times—49 sts.

Continue even in the pattern as established until the hood measures approximately 4½ in/11 cm from the beginning, ending after a WS row.

Next Row (RS) (Decrease Row): Work the pattern as established until 2 sts before the marked st, ssk, k1 (the marked st), k2tog, work the pattern as established across to end of row—47 sts remain.

Work 3 rows even in the pattern, keeping the center st as knit on the RS and purl on the WS.

Repeat the last 4 rows 4 more times—39 sts remain.

Next Row (WS): Work even in the pattern as established.

Next Row: Work the Decrease Row—37 sts remain.

Repeat the last 2 rows once more—35 sts remain.

Next Row (WS): Work the pattern as established across the first 17 sts, p2tog, work the pattern as established across to end the row—34 sts remain.

BO.

Fold the bound-off edge in half, and use mattress stitch to seam 17 sts to 17 sts for the top of the hood.

Sew the sleeve caps into the armholes, aligning the bound-off edges and centering the top of the sleeve caps on the shoulder seams.

Sew the side and sleeve seams. Hide yarn tails.

Using the sharp needle and matching thread, sew on the buttons opposite the buttonholes, alternating colors as seen in the photograph.

KNITTING KNOW-HOW

WORKING IN SEED STITCH

Seed stitch is one of the workhorse stitch patterns used in knitting. Because knit stitches are always worked in purl stitches, and vice versa, the fabric does not curl at the edges. It's perfect for jackets and other projects when a borderless, "no-edge" edge is desired. When you increase or decrease the number of stitches, remember to knit the purls and purl the knits and you won't have any trouble keeping the pattern lined up.

CHANGE IT UP!

If you would prefer a collar instead of a hood, pick up and knit the same number of stitches around the neck edge that are called for in the pattern. Begin the Seed Stitch Pattern, and use the kf&b technique to increase one stitch at the beginning and end of every other row until the collar is the desired length. Bind off in the pattern to finish.

On Neutral Ground

CROPPED JACKET

Here's a little jacket that's short, sweet, and super easy to knit. The textured knit/purl pattern means that the edges don't curl, so there's very little finishing to do. The collar adds the perfect touch. Score!

SKILL SET: *Cable cast on (page 20)* • *Knit stitch (page 21)* • *Purl stitch (page 24)* • *Binding off (page 40)* • *K2tog decrease (page 26)* • *Hiding yarn tails (page 48)* • *Blocking (page 44)* • *Mattress stitch seams (page 44)* • *Picking up and knitting (page 42)*

SIZES

Women's S(M, L, 1X, 2X, 3X). Instructions are for the smallest size, with changes for other sizes noted in parentheses as necessary.

FINISHED MEASUREMENTS

Bust: 35(39, 43, 47, 51, 55) in/89(99, 109, 119, 129.5, 140) cm

Length: 18(18½, 19, 19, 19½, 19½) in/ 45.5(47, 48, 48, 49.5, 49.5) cm

YARN

» Lion Brand/Martha Stewart Crafts *Extra Soft Wool Blend* (3-light/DK weight; 65% acrylic/35% wool; 164 yd/150 m per 3½ oz/100 g): 7(8, 9, 10, 11, 12) balls

Shown in Buttermilk #599

NEEDLES

US 6/4 mm knitting needles

NOTIONS

Safety pin

Blunt-end yarn needle

Sharp sewing needle

Matching sewing thread

2 buttons, 1½-in/4-cm diameter (shown with JHB International's Squiggles #550043 in Brown)

GAUGE

24 stitches and 28 rows per 4 in/10 cm in the Nubby Pattern, blocked

To save time, take time to check gauge.

PATTERN NOTE

» This jacket is knit in four pieces from the bottom up.

STITCH PATTERN

Nubby Pattern (over a multiple of 2 sts +1 st):

Rows 1 and 3 (RS): *P1, k1; repeat from the * across, ending with p1.

Row 2: *K1, p1; repeat from the * across, ending with k1.

Row 4: *P1, k1; repeat from the * across, ending with p1.

Repeat Rows 1 through 4 for the pattern.

BACK

Use the cable cast-on technique to CO 107(119, 131, 143, 155, 167) sts.

Begin the Nubby Pattern, and work even until the piece measures approximately 10 in/25.5 cm from the beginning, ending after WS row.

SHAPE ARMHOLES

BO 4(5, 6, 7, 8, 9) sts at the beginning of the next 2 rows.

BO 2(2, 3, 3, 4, 5) sts at the beginning of the next 2 rows.

Use the k2tog technique to decrease 1 st at the beginning and end of every row 2(6, 4, 8, 10, 12) times.

Decrease 1 st at the beginning and end of every RS row 4(3, 5, 4, 4, 4) times—83(87, 95, 99, 103, 107) sts remain.

Continue even in the pattern as established until the piece measures approximately 17(17½, 18, 18, 18½, 18½) in/43(44.5, 45.5, 45.5, 47, 47) cm, ending after WS row.

SHAPE SHOULDERS

BO 7(8, 9, 10, 11, 11) sts at the beginning of the next 4 rows.

BO 8(8, 10, 10, 10, 12) sts at the beginning of the next 2 rows.

BO the remaining 39 sts in the pattern.

LEFT FRONT

Use the cable cast-on technique to CO 59(65, 71, 77, 83, 89) sts.

Begin the Nubby Pattern, and work even until the piece measures approximately 10 in/25.5 cm from the beginning, ending after a WS row.

SHAPE ARMHOLE

Next Row (RS): BO 4(5, 6, 7, 8, 9) sts, work in pattern to the end of the row.

Next Row (WS): Work even in the pattern as established.

Next Row (RS): BO 2(2, 3, 3, 4, 5) sts, work in pattern to the end of the row.

Next Row (WS Decrease Row): Work in pattern to the last 3 sts, k2tog, k1.

Next Row (RS Decrease Row): K1, k2tog, work in pattern to the end of the row.

Repeat the last 2 rows 0(2, 1, 3, 4, 5) times.

Repeat the RS Decrease Row every 4 rows 4(3, 5, 4, 4, 4) times—47(49, 53, 55, 57, 59) sts remain.

Continue even in the pattern as established until the piece measures approximately 15(15½, 16, 16, 16½, 16½) in/38(39.5, 40.5, 40.5, 42, 42) cm from the beginning, ending after a RS row.

SHAPE NECK

Next Row (WS): BO 12 sts, work in pattern to the end of the row.

Work 1 row even.

Next Row: BO 4 sts at the neck edge, work in pattern to the end of the row.

Work 1 row even.

BO 3 sts, work to the end of the row.

Work 1 row even.

Repeat the last 2 rows once more.

Use the k2tog technique to decrease 1 st at the neck edge every row 3 times—22(24, 28, 30, 32, 34) sts remain.

Continue even in the pattern as established until the piece measures the same as the back to the beginning of the shoulder, ending after a WS row.

Continued...

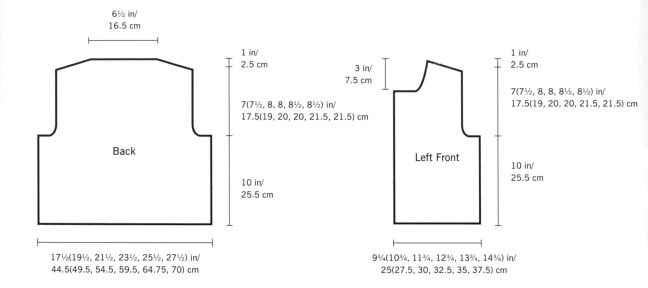

6½ in/
16.5 cm

1 in/
2.5 cm

3 in/
7.5 cm

1 in/
2.5 cm

7(7½, 8, 8, 8½, 8½) in/
17.5(19, 20, 20, 21.5, 21.5) cm

7(7½, 8, 8, 8½, 8½) in/
17.5(19, 20, 20, 21.5, 21.5) cm

Back

Left Front

10 in/
25.5 cm

10 in/
25.5 cm

17½(19½, 21½, 23½, 25½, 27½) in/
44.5(49.5, 54.5, 59.5, 64.75, 70) cm

9¾(10¾, 11¾, 12¾, 13¾, 14¾) in/
25(27.5, 30, 32.5, 35, 37.5) cm

SHAPE SHOULDER

BO 7(8, 9, 10, 11, 11) sts at the shoulder edge.

Work 1 row even.

Repeat the last 2 rows once.

Work 1 row even.

BO the remaining 8(8, 10, 10, 10, 12) sts.

Place a marker ½ in/1.5 cm down from the beginning of the front neck shaping.

RIGHT FRONT

Use the cable cast-on technique to CO 59(65, 71, 77, 83, 89) sts.

Begin the Nubby Pattern, and work even until the piece measures approximately 10 in/25.5 cm from the beginning, ending after a RS row.

SHAPE ARMHOLE

Next Row (WS): BO 4(5, 6, 7, 8, 9) sts, work in pattern to the end of the row.

Work 1 row even.

Next Row: BO 2(2, 3, 3, 4, 5) sts, work to the end of the row in pattern.

Use the k2tog technique to decrease 1 st at the armhole edge every row 2(6, 4, 8, 10, 12) times, then every RS row 4(3, 5, 4, 4, 4) times—47(49, 53, 55, 57, 59) sts remain.

Continue even in the pattern as established until the piece measures the height where the marker is placed on the left front, ending after a WS row.

Next Row (RS) (Buttonhole Row): Work 4 sts in the pattern as established, BO 5 sts, continue the pattern across to the end of the row.

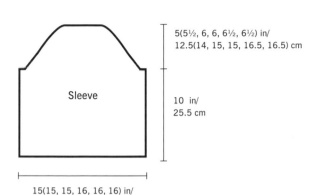

5(5½, 6, 6, 6½, 6½) in/
12.5(14, 15, 15, 16.5, 16.5) cm

Sleeve

10 in/
25.5 cm

15(15, 15, 16, 16, 16) in/
38(38, 38, 40.5, 40.5, 40.5) cm

Next Row: Work the pattern as established across to the bound-off sts of the previous row, use the cable cast-on technique to CO 5 sts, continue the pattern across to the end of the row.

Continue even in the pattern as established until the piece measures approximately 15(15½, 16, 16, 16½, 16½) in/38(39.5, 40.5, 40.5, 42, 42) cm from the beginning, ending after a WS row.

SHAPE NECK

Next Row (RS): BO 12 sts, work in pattern to the end of the row.

Work 1 row even.

Next Row: BO 4 sts at the neck edge, work in pattern to the end of the row.

Work 1 row even.

BO 3 sts, work to the end of the row.

Work 1 row even.

Repeat the last 2 rows once more.

Use the k2tog technique to decrease 1 st at the neck edge every row 3 times—22(24, 28, 30, 32, 34) sts remain.

Continue even in the pattern as established until the piece measures same as the back to the beginning of the shoulder, ending after a RS row.

SHAPE SHOULDER

BO 7(8, 9, 10, 11, 11) sts at the shoulder edge.

Work 1 row even.

Repeat the last 2 rows once.

Work 1 row even.

BO the remaining 8(8, 10, 10, 10, 12) sts.

SLEEVES (MAKE 2)

Use the cable cast-on technique to CO 91(91, 91, 97, 97, 97) sts.

Begin the Nubby Pattern, and work even until the piece measures approximately 10 in/25.5 cm from the beginning, ending after a WS row.

SHAPE SLEEVE CAP

BO 4(5, 6, 7, 8, 9) sts at the beginning of the next 2 rows, then use the k2tog technique to decrease 1 st at the beginning and end of every RS row 3(8, 12, 10, 15, 16) times, then every row 22(16, 11, 15, 9, 7) times—33 sts.

BO 3 sts at the beginning of the next 4 rows—21 sts.

BO all sts.

Continued…

FINISHING

Hide yarn tails.

Block to the finished measurements.

Use mattress stitch to sew the shoulder seams.

NECKBAND

Beginning at the right front neck edge with the RS facing, pick up and knit 99 sts along neckline.

Beginning with Row 2 of the Nubby Pattern, work in pattern until the neckband measures approximately 2½ in/6 cm from the beginning, ending after a WS row.

Buttonhole Row (RS): Work the pattern as established across the first 4 sts, BO the next 5 sts, work in pattern as established across to the end of the row.

Next Row: Work the pattern as established across to the bound-off sts in the previous row, use the cable cast-on technique to CO 5 sts, continue in pattern across to the end of the row.

Continue even in the pattern as established until the neckband measures approximately 3½ in/9 cm from the beginning.

BO all sts in pattern.

Position the sleeve caps into the armholes with the center of the sleeve at the shoulder seams and the edges of the body pieces and the sleeves aligned. Sew them into place.

Sew the sleeve and side seams.

Using the sharp needle and matching thread, sew on the buttons opposite the buttonholes.

CHANGE IT UP!

If you'd prefer buttons all the way down the front of the jacket, place markers evenly along the left front, putting the last approximately ½ in/1.5 cm from the lower edge and the first the same distance from the beginning of the front neck shaping. Make buttonholes on the right front opposite each marker by following the pattern instructions for the Buttonhole Row.

Dress Me Up

LITTLE GIRL'S DRESS

This adorable dress is perfect for the little girl in your life. Its empire waist and ribbon tie make it delightfully ladylike. Best of all, it requires only basic knitting skills! She'll love it—and you.

SKILL SET: *Cable cast on (page 20) • Knit stitch (page 21) • Purl stitch (page 24) • K2tog decrease (page 26) • M1 knitwise (page 29), ssk decrease (page 26), and yarn-over increase (page 27) • Binding off (page 40) • Hiding yarn tails (page 48) • Blocking (page 44) • Mattress stitch seams (page 44) • Picking up and knitting (page 42)*

SIZES

Child's Size 2(4, 6). Instructions are for the smallest size, with changes for other sizes noted in parentheses as necessary.

FINISHED MEASUREMENTS

Chest: 22(24, 26) in/56(60.5, 66) cm

Hip: 34(36, 38) in/86(91, 96) cm

Length: 20(21, 22½) in/50(53.5, 57) cm

YARN

» Plymouth Yarn *Worsted Merino Superwash* (4-medium/worsted weight; 100% superwash wool; 218 yd/199 m per 3½ oz/100 g): For all sizes, 3 hanks MC, 2 hanks CC

Shown in Lavender #18 [MC] and Violet #34 [CC]

NEEDLES

US 5/3.75 mm knitting needles

US 7/4.5 mm knitting needles (or size needed to obtain gauge)

NOTIONS

2 stitch holders

Blunt-end yarn needle

Sharp sewing needle

Matching sewing thread

Three ⅜-in/1-cm diameter buttons (shown with JHB International's Pearl Balls #10911 in White)

1 piece of ribbon, 1 in/2.5 cm wide and 50 in/127 cm long, for tie

GAUGE

20 stitches and 28 rows per 4 in/10 cm in St St, blocked, with the larger needles

To save time, take time to check gauge.

PATTERN NOTES

» This dress is knit in four pieces from the bottom up.

» For fully fashioned decreases: On RS rows, k2, ssk, work in pattern to last 4 sts, end row with k2tog, k2. On WS rows, p2, p2tog, work to last 4 sts, end row with p2tog, p2.

» For fully fashioned increases: On RS rows, k2, M1 knitwise, knit to last 2 sts, end row with M1 knitwise, k2.

STITCH PATTERNS

Garter Stitch Pattern (over any number of sts):

Row 1 (RS): Knit across.

Pattern Row: As Row 1.

Stockinette Stitch Pattern (over any number of sts):

Row 1 (RS): Knit across.

Row 2: Purl across.

Repeat Rows 1 and 2 for the pattern.

BACK

With the smaller needles and MC, use the cable cast-on technique to CO 74(77, 82) sts.

Begin Garter Stitch Pattern, and work even until the piece measures approximately 1 in/2.5 cm from the beginning, ending after a RS row.

Next Row (WS): K2(1, 1), *k5, M1; repeat from the * to last 7(6, 6) sts, knit to the end of the row—87(91, 97) sts.

Change to larger needles, and work even in St St until the piece measures approximately 13½ (14½, 15½) in/34(37, 39.5) cm from the beginning, ending after a WS row.

DECREASE FOR EMPIRE WAISTBAND

For size 2 only:
Next Row: K1, [k2tog, k1] 5 times, [k2tog] 28 times, [k1, k2tog] 5 times—49 sts remain.

For size 4 only:
Next Row: K1, [k2tog, k1] 6 times, [k2tog] 28 times, [k1, k2tog] 5 times, k1—52 sts remain.

For size 6 only:
Next Row: [K2tog, k1] 9 times, [k2tog] 23 times, [k1, k2tog] 8 times—57 sts remain.

Continue even in Garter Stitch Pattern until the piece measures approximately 14½ (15½, 16½) in/37(39.5, 42) cm from the beginning, ending after a WS row.

INCREASE FOR YOKE

For size 2 only:
Next Row: [K6, M1] 8 times, k1—57 sts.

For size 4 only:
Next Row: K1, [k5, M1] 9 times, k6—61 sts.

For size 6 only:
Next Row: K1, [k5, M1] 10 times, k6—67 sts.

Continue even until the piece measures approximately 15½ (16, 17) in/39.5(40.5, 43) cm from the beginning, ending after a WS row.

SHAPE ARMHOLES

BO 2(2, 3) sts at the beginning of the next 2 rows.

BO 2 sts at the beginning of the next 2 rows.

Work fully fashioned decreases (see Pattern Notes) at the beginning and end of every RS row 1 (2, 3) times—47(49, 51) sts remain.

Continue even until the piece measures approximately 19½ (20½, 22) in/49.5(52, 56) cm from the beginning, ending after a WS row.

SHAPE NECK

Next Row (RS): K12(13, 14) sts, join a second ball of yarn and BO the middle 23 sts, knit to the end of the row.

Work 1 row even, switching balls of yarn at neck.

Next Row (RS): Work to last 3 sts before neck edge, k2tog, k1; switch yarns and k1, k2tog, work to the end of the row—11(12, 13) sts remain each side.

Work 1 WS row even. The piece should measure approximately 20(21, 22½) in/50(53.5, 57) cm from the beginning.

Next Row (RS): BO 11(12, 13) sts for the right shoulder; slip the remaining 11(12, 13) sts onto a holder for the left shoulder.

Continued…

FRONT

Cast on and work the same as the back through the armhole shaping until the piece measures approximately 17(18, 19½) in/43(45.5, 49.5) cm from the beginning, ending after a WS row.

SHAPE NECK

Next Row (RS): K18(19, 20) sts, join a second ball of yarn and BO the middle 11 sts, knit to the end of the row.

Work both sides at once with separate balls of yarn, and BO 3 sts each neck edge once, BO 2 sts each neck edge once, then use the k2tog technique to decrease 1 st each neck edge every RS row twice—11(12, 13) sts remain each side.

Continue even until the front measures the same as the back, ending after a WS row.

Next Row (RS): Slip 11(12, 13) sts to a holder for the left shoulder; BO 11(12, 13) right shoulder sts.

SLEEVES (MAKE 2)

With the smaller needles and MC, use the cable cast-on technique to CO 42 sts.

Begin Garter Stitch Pattern, and work even until the piece measures approximately 1 in/2.5 cm from the beginning, ending after RS row.

Next Row (WS): K3, [M1, k6] 6 times, M1, k3— 49 sts.

Change to larger needles, begin St St, and work fully fashioned increases (see Pattern Notes) every RS row 1(1, 3) times—51(51, 55) sts.

Continue even until the piece measures approximately 1½(1½, 2) in/4(4, 5) cm from the beginning, ending after a WS row.

SHAPE SLEEVE CAP

BO 2(2, 3) sts at the beginning of the next 2 rows, then work fully fashioned decreases each side every RS row 8(8, 7) times, then every row 4(4, 6) times—23 sts remain.

Work 1 row even.

BO 3 sts at the beginning of the next 4 rows.

BO remaining 11 sts.

FINISHING

Hide yarn tails.

Block to the finished measurements.

Sew right shoulder seam.

NECKBAND

Using the smaller needles and MC, with RS facing, pick up and knit 86 sts along the neckline.

Begin Garter Stitch Pattern, and work even until the neckband measures approximately 1 in/2.5 cm from the beginning.

BO on a RS row.

BUTTON BAND

With the smaller needles and MC, pick up and knit 5 sts along the side of neckband, then knit the 11(12, 13) sts from the back left shoulder holder—16(17, 18) sts total.

Begin Garter Stitch Pattern, and work even until the band measures approximately 1 in/2.5 cm from the beginning.

BO on a RS row.

Continued...

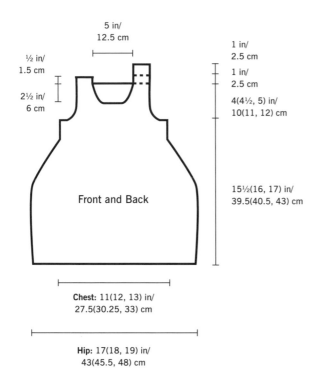

5 in/
12.5 cm

½ in/
1.5 cm

2½ in/
6 cm

1 in/
2.5 cm

1 in/
2.5 cm

4(4½, 5) in/
10(11, 12) cm

Front and Back

15½(16, 17) in/
39.5(40.5, 43) cm

Chest: 11(12, 13) in/
27.5(30.25, 33) cm

Hip: 17(18, 19) in/
43(45.5, 48) cm

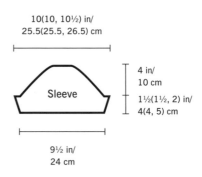

10(10, 10½) in/
25.5(25.5, 26.5) cm

4 in/
10 cm

Sleeve

1½(1½, 2) in/
4(4, 5) cm

9½ in/
24 cm

BUTTONHOLE BAND

Knit the 11(12, 13) sts from the holder for the front left shoulder, then pick up and knit 5 sts from the neckband. Work in Garter Stitch Pattern until the band measures approximately ½ in/1.5 cm from the beginning, ending with a WS row.

Next Row (RS): Make 3 buttonholes as follows: K3(4, 4), *yo, k2tog, k2; repeat from the * 3 times, ending with k1(1, 2).

Complete as for the button band.

Overlap the buttonhole band over the button band and use mattress stitch to sew the ends together at the armhole edge.

Set the sleeve caps into the armholes with the center of the sleeve at the shoulder seams and the edges of the body pieces and the sleeves aligned. Sew them into place.

Sew the sleeve and side seams.

RIBBON TIE

Cut the ribbon into two 24-in/60.5-cm lengths. Sew onto the side seams at the contrasting garter stitch band.

Using the sharp needle and matching thread, sew on the buttons in the middle of the button band opposite the buttonholes.

CHANGE IT UP!

For a playful, color-block look, try working the skirt, bodice, and sleeves in different colors.

The Big Easy

CABLED PULLOVER

This classic pullover is perfect for any wardrobe. The reverse stockinette stitch background is easy, the center staghorn cable adds visual interest without much effort—and the thick-and-thin wool makes it speedy! Make tick marks to keep careful track of which pattern row you're on.

SKILL SET: *Cable cast on (page 20) • Knit stitch (page 21) • Purl stitch (page 24) • Cables (page 32) • P2tog decrease (page 27) and k2tog decrease (page 26) • M1 purlwise increase (page 29) • Binding off (page 40) • Hiding yarn tails (page 48) • Blocking (page 44) • Mattress stitch seams (page 44) • Picking up and knitting (page 42)*

SIZES

Women's Small(Medium, Large, 1X, 2X, 3X). Instructions are for the smallest size, with changes for other sizes noted in parentheses as necessary.

FINISHED MEASUREMENTS

Bust: 35(39, 43, 47, 51, 55) in/89(99, 109, 119, 129.5, 140) cm

Hip: 32(36, 40, 44, 48, 52) in/81(91, 102, 112, 122, 132) cm

Length: 24(24½, 25, 25½, 25½, 26) in/60.5(62, 63.5, 64.75, 64.75, 66) cm

YARN

» Cascade Yarns *Jewel Hand Dyed* (5-bulky weight; 100% wool; 142 yd/130 m per 3½ oz/100 g): 7(7, 8, 9, 9, 10) hanks

Shown in Charcoal #9264

NEEDLES

US 8/5 mm knitting needles

US 10/6 mm knitting needles (or size needed to obtain gauge)

Cable needle

NOTIONS

2 stitch markers

Blunt-end yarn needle

GAUGE

15 stitches and 22 rows per 4 in/10 cm in Rev St St, blocked, with the larger needles

The 16-stitch Cable Panel measures 3 in/7.5 cm across, blocked, with the larger needles.

To save time, take time to check gauge.

PATTERN NOTES

» This sweater is knit in four pieces from the bottom up.

» To ensure random color distribution, work from two different balls of yarn, alternating two rows from each.

» The instructions include one selvedge stitch on each side for seaming; these stitches are not reflected in the final measurements.

» For fully fashioned increases: P1, M1 purlwise, work in patterns as established across to last stitch, M1 purlwise, p1.

» For fully fashioned decreases: On RS rows: P1, p2tog, work in patterns as established across to last 3 sts, p2tog, p1. On WS rows: K1, k2tog, work in patterns as established across to last 3 sts, k2tog, k1.

STITCH PATTERNS

K1P1 Rib Pattern (over a multiple of 2 sts):

Row 1 (RS): *K1, p1; repeat from the * across.

Pattern Row: As Row 1 (you will be knitting the knit stitches and purling the purl stitches).

Reverse Stockinette Stitch (Rev St St) (over any number of stitches):

Row 1 (RS): Purl.

Row 2: Knit.

Repeat Rows 1 and 2 for the pattern.

Cable Panel (over 16 sts):

Row 1 (RS): K4, slip the next 2 sts onto cn (cable needle) and hold it in back, k2, k2 from the cn, slip the next 2 sts onto cn and hold it in front, k2, k2 from the cn, k4.

Row 2 and all WS rows: Purl across.

Row 3: K2, slip the next 2 sts onto cn and hold it in back, k2, k2 from the cn, k4, slip the next 2 sts onto cn and hold it in front, k2, k2 from the cn, k2.

Row 5: Slip the next 2 sts onto cn and hold it in back, k2, k2 from the cn, k8, slip the next 2 sts onto cn and hold it in front, k2, k2 from the cn.

Row 6: As Row 2.

Repeat Rows 1 through 6 for the pattern.

BACK

With the smaller needles, use the cable cast-on technique to CO 62(70, 78, 84, 92, 100) sts.

Begin the K1P1 Rib Pattern, and work even until the piece measures approximately 2 in/5 cm from the beginning, ending after a WS row.

Next Row (RS): Work 25(29, 33, 36, 40, 44) sts in pattern, place marker to indicate the cable section, work 12 center sts, place marker, work in pattern to the end of the row.

Next Row (WS): Work to the first marker in pattern, slip the marker, [work 3 sts in pattern, M1 purlwise] 4 times, slip the second marker, work pattern as established to the end of the row—66(74, 82, 88, 96, 104) sts.

SET UP THE PATTERNS

Next Row (RS): Change to the larger needles, work Row 1 of Rev St St across the first 25(29, 33, 36, 40, 44) sts, slip the marker, work Row 1 of the Cable Panel across the middle 16 sts, slip the marker, work Row 1 of Rev St St to the end of the row.

Continue to work in patterns as established, and, *at the same time*, work fully fashioned increases (see Pattern Notes) at the beginning and end of the row every 20 rows 3 times—72(80, 88, 94, 102, 110) sts.

Continue to work even in the patterns as established until the piece measures approximately 15½ in/39 cm from the beginning, ending after a WS row.

SHAPE ARMHOLES

BO 2(3, 3, 4, 4, 5) sts at the beginning of the next 2 rows, BO 2(2, 3, 3, 3, 4) sts at the beginning of the next 2 rows, then work fully fashioned decreases (see Pattern Notes) every row 1(2, 4, 3, 5, 4) times, then every RS row 3(3, 3, 4, 4, 5) times—56(60, 62, 66, 70, 74) sts remain.

KNITTING KNOW-HOW

CABLES
Cables naturally draw the fabric in widthwise. To prevent the lower edge of the sweater from flaring beneath the cabled section, stitches are increased in that area.

Continue to work even in the patterns as established until the piece measures approximately 22½(23, 23½, 24, 24, 24½) in/57(58, 59.5, 60.5, 60.5, 62) cm from the beginning, ending after WS row. The back cable panel is complete.

SHAPE NECK

Next Row (RS): Work in pattern as established across the first 13(15, 16, 18, 20, 22) sts, join a second ball of yarn and BO the middle 30 sts, work across to end of row.

Work both sides at once with separate balls of yarn, and use the p2tog technique to decrease 1 st each neck edge once on the next RS row—12(14, 15, 17, 19, 21) sts remain on each side.

Work 1 WS row.

SHAPE SHOULDERS

NOTE: *These instructions describe working both shoulders as one row; you will drop one ball of yarn and pick up the second mid-row.*

BO 4 (5, 5, 6, 6, 7) sts at the beginning of the next 4 rows, then BO 4 (4, 5, 5, 7, 7) sts at the beginning of the next 2 rows.

Continued…

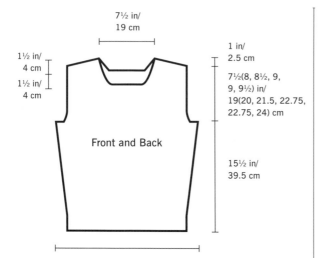

7½ in/ 19 cm

1 in/ 2.5 cm

7½(8, 8½, 9, 9, 9½) in/ 19(20, 21.5, 22.75, 22.75, 24) cm

1½ in/ 4 cm

1½ in/ 4 cm

15½ in/ 39.5 cm

Front and Back

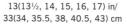

Bust: 17½(19½, 21½, 23½, 25½, 27½) in/ 44.5(49.5, 54.5, 59.5, 64.75, 70) cm

Hip: 16(18, 20, 22, 24, 26) in/ 40.5(45.5, 50, 56, 60.5, 66) cm

13(13½, 14, 15, 16, 17) in/ 33(34, 35.5, 38, 40.5, 43) cm

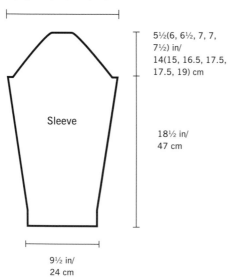

5½(6, 6½, 7, 7, 7½) in/ 14(15, 16.5, 17.5, 17.5, 19) cm

Sleeve

18½ in/ 47 cm

9½ in/ 24 cm

FRONT

Work the same as the back through the armhole shaping until the piece measures approximately 21(21½, 22, 22½, 22½, 23) in/53.5(54.5, 56, 57, 57, 58) cm from the beginning, ending after a WS row. The front cable panel is complete.

SHAPE NECK

Next Row (RS): Work in pattern as established across the first 21(23, 24, 26, 28, 30) sts, join a second ball of yarn and BO the middle 14 sts, work to end of row.

Work both sides at once with separate balls of yarn, and BO 3 sts at each neck edge once, BO 2 sts at each neck edge twice, then use the p2tog technique to decrease 1 st at each neck edge once—12(14, 15, 17, 19, 21) sts remain for each shoulder.

Work even until the piece measures approximately 23(23½, 24, 24½, 24½, 25) in/58(59.5, 60.5, 62, 62, 63.5) cm from the beginning, or the same as the back to the beginning of shoulder shaping, ending after a WS row.

SHAPE SHOULDERS

BO 4(5, 5, 6, 6, 7) sts at the beginning of the next 4 rows, then BO 4(4, 5, 5, 7, 7) sts at the beginning of the next 2 rows.

SLEEVES (MAKE 2)

With the smaller needles, CO 38 sts.

Begin the K1P1 Rib Pattern, and work even until the piece measures approximately 2 in/5 cm from the beginning, ending after WS row.

Change to larger needles, begin Rev St St, and work fully fashioned increases at the beginning and end of every 6 rows 0(0, 0, 0, 5, 13) times, every 8 rows 0(0, 0, 7, 7, 1) times, every 10 rows 0(0, 5, 3, 0, 0) times, every 12 rows 0(6, 3, 0, 0, 0) times, every 14 rows 5(1, 0, 0, 0, 0) times, then every 16 rows 1(0, 0, 0, 0, 0) time—50(52, 54, 58, 62, 66) sts.

Continue even until the piece measures approximately 18½ in/47 cm from the beginning, ending after a WS row.

SHAPE SLEEVE CAP

BO 2(3, 3, 4, 4, 5) sts at the beginning of the next 2 rows, then work fully fashioned decreases (see Pattern Notes) at the beginning and end of every 4 rows 0(0, 0, 1, 0, 0) time, every other row 11(13, 14, 14, 15, 17) times, then every row 2(0, 0, 0, 2, 1) times—20 sts remain. Work 0(0, 1, 0, 0, 0) row even.

BO.

FINISHING

Hide yarn tails.

Block to the finished measurements.

Use mattress stitch to sew right shoulder seam, but leave left shoulder seam open.

NECKBAND

Using smaller needles and with RS facing, start at left front shoulder and pick up and knit 88 sts along neckline.

Work K1P1 Rib Pattern until the neckband measures approximately 1 in/2.5 cm.

BO *loosely* in pattern.

Use mattress stitch to sew the left shoulder seam, including the side of the neckband.

Sew in the sleeves.

Sew the side and sleeve seams.

CHANGE IT UP!

For a more contemporary, fuller sleeve, cast on the total number of stitches at the get-go and work even up to the sleeve cap without increasing.

Boss Tweed

MAN'S CASUAL SWEATER

This sweater works up quickly in a super soft alpaca-blend yarn. Your man will love it—and you, too, of course, for making it for him! The color pattern is really simple to do using just one color per row and slipped stitches.

SKILL SET: *Cable cast on (page 20)* • *Knit stitch (page 21)* • *Attaching a new yarn ball (page 25)* • *Purl stitch (page 24)* • *Binding off (page 40)* • *M1 knitwise (page 29)* • *P2tog decrease (page 27)* • *K2tog decrease (page 26)* • *Hiding yarn tails (page 48)* • *Blocking (page 44)* • *Mattress stitch seams (page 44)* • *Picking up and knitting (page 42)*

SIZES

Men's S(M, L, XL, XXL). Instructions are for the smallest size, with changes for other sizes noted in parentheses as necessary.

FINISHED MEASUREMENTS

Chest: 42(46, 50, 54, 58) in/107(117, 127, 137, 148) cm

Length: 26(26½, 26½, 27, 27½) in/66(67, 67, 68.5, 70) cm

YARN

» Cascade Yarns *Cloud* (4-medium/worsted weight; 70% merino wool/30% baby alpaca; 164 yd/150 m per 3½ oz/100 g): 6(7, 8, 8, 9) hanks MC

» Cascade Yarns *Eco Cloud* (4-medium/ worsted weight; 70% merino wool/30% baby alpaca; 164 yd/150 m per 3½ oz/100 g): 3(4, 4, 5, 5) hanks CC

Shown in Navy #2119 [MC] and Pearl #1809 [CC]

NEEDLES

US 8/5 mm knitting needles

US 10/6 mm knitting needles (or size needed to obtain gauge)

NOTIONS

Blunt-end yarn needle

GAUGE

18 stitches and 32 rows per 4 in/10 cm in Bird's Eye Pattern, blocked, with the larger needles

To save time, take time to check gauge.

PATTERN NOTES

» This sweater is knit in four pieces from the bottom up.

» For fully fashioned increases: K1, M1 knitwise with the working yarn, work in patterns as established across to the last stitch, M1 knitwise, k1.

» When changing color, don't cut the yarn at the end of the stripes; instead, carry it loosely up the side of the fabric until it is needed again.

STITCH PATTERNS

K2P2 Rib Pattern (over a multiple of 4 sts + 2 sts):

Row 1 (RS): *K2, p2; repeat from the * across, ending the row with k2.

Row 2: *P2, k2; repeat from the * across, ending the row with p2.

Repeat Rows 1 and 2 for the pattern.

Bird's Eye Pattern (over a multiple of 2 sts + 1 st):

Row 1 (RS): With MC, knit across.

Row 2: With MC, purl across.

Row 3: With CC, k1, *slip the next st purlwise with yarn in back, k1; repeat from the * across.

Row 4: With CC, k1, *slip the next st purlwise with yarn in front, k1; repeat from the * across.

Rows 5 and 6: With MC, as Rows 1 and 2.

Row 7: With CC, k2, *slip the next st purlwise with yarn in back, k1; repeat from the * across, ending with k1.

Row 8: With CC, k2, *slip the next st purlwise with yarn in front, k1; repeat from the * across, ending with k1.

Repeat Rows 1 through 8 for pattern.

BACK

With the smaller needles and CC, use the cable cast-on technique to CO 94(102, 110, 118, 126) sts.

Change to MC, begin the K2P2 Rib Pattern, and work even until the piece measures approximately 2½ in/6 cm from the beginning, ending after WS row.

For size S only:
Next Row (RS): Change to the larger needles, [k31, M1] 3 times, k1—97 sts.

For size M only:
Next Row (RS): Change to the larger needles, k1, [M1, k33] twice, M1, k35—105 sts.

For size L only:
Next Row (RS): Change to the larger needles, k1, [M1, k22] 4 times, M1, k21—115 sts.

For size XL only:
Next Row (RS): Change to the larger needles, k3, [M1, k23] 4 times, M1, k23—123 sts.

For size XXL only:
Next Row (RS): Change to the larger needles, k1, [M1, k18] 6 times, M1, k17—133 sts.

Begin with Row 2 of the Bird's Eye Pattern, and continue even in the pattern until the piece measures approximately 15¾ in/40 cm from the beginning, ending after a WS row.

SHAPE ARMHOLES

BO 10(12, 14, 18, 22) sts at the beginning of the next 2 rows—77(81, 87, 87, 89) sts remain.

Continue even in the pattern as established until the piece measures approximately 24½(25, 25, 25½, 26) in/62(63.5, 63.5, 64.75, 66) cm from the beginning, ending after WS row.

SHAPE NECK

Next Row (RS): Work the first 22(24, 27, 27, 28) sts in pattern, join a second ball of yarn and BO the middle 33 sts with the working yarn, work in pattern to the end of the row.

Work both sides at once with separate balls of yarn, and use the p2tog technique to decrease 1 st at each neck edge once—21(23, 26, 26, 27) sts remain on each side.

Continue even in the patterns as established until the piece measures approximately 25(25½, 25½, 26, 26½) in/63.5(64.75, 64.75, 66, 67) cm from the beginning, ending after a WS row.

SHAPE SHOULDERS

BO 5(6, 7, 7, 7) sts at the beginning of the next 6 rows, then BO 6(5, 5, 5, 6) sts at the beginning of the next 2 rows.

Continued…

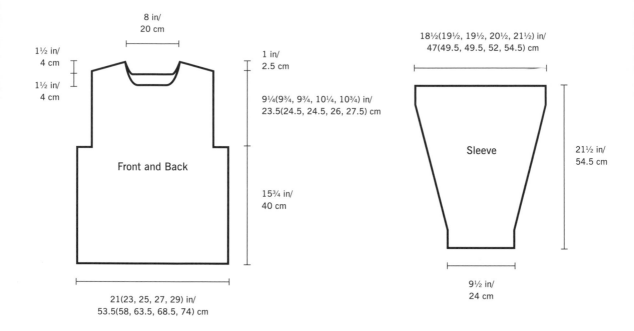

Front and Back diagram: 8 in/20 cm, 1½ in/4 cm, 1½ in/4 cm, 1 in/2.5 cm, 9¼(9¾, 9¾, 10¼, 10¾) in/23.5(24.5, 24.5, 26, 27.5) cm, 15¾ in/40 cm, 21(23, 25, 27, 29) in/53.5(58, 63.5, 68.5, 74) cm

Sleeve diagram: 18½(19½, 19½, 20½, 21½) in/47(49.5, 49.5, 52, 54.5) cm, 21½ in/54.5 cm, 9½ in/24 cm

FRONT

Work the same as the back through the armhole shaping until the piece measures approximately 23(23½, 23½, 24, 24½) in/58(59.5, 59.5, 60.5, 62) cm from the beginning, ending after a WS row.

SHAPE NECK

Next Row (RS): Work pattern as established across the first 31(33, 36, 36, 37) sts, join a second ball of yarn and BO the middle 15 sts, work across to the end of the row.

Work both sides at once with separate balls of yarn, and BO 5 sts at each neck edge once, BO 2 sts at each neck edge twice, then use the k2tog technique to decrease at each neck edge once—21(23, 26, 26, 27) sts remain on each side.

Continue even in the patterns as established until the piece measures approximately 25(25½, 25½, 26, 26½) in/63.5(64.75, 64.75, 66, 67) cm from the beginning, ending after a WS row.

SHAPE SHOULDERS

Same as for back.

SLEEVES (MAKE 2)

With the smaller needles and MC, use the cable cast-on technique to CO 42 sts.

Begin the K2P2 Rib Pattern, and work even until the piece measures approximately 2½ in/6 cm from the beginning, ending after WS row.

Next Row (RS): Change to the larger needles, K1, [M1, k14] twice, M1, k13—45 sts.

Begin with Row 2 of the Bird's Eye Pattern, and *at the same time,* use the M1 knitwise technique to increase 1 st at the beginning and end of RS rows every 4 rows 0(0, 2, 15, 25) times, every 6 rows 13(22, 20, 10, 2) times, then every 8 rows 7(0, 0, 0, 0) times. Work new stitches into the pattern as you go—85(89, 89, 95, 99) sts.

Continue even until the piece measures approximately 21½ in/54.5 cm from the beginning, ending after a WS row.

BO all sts.

FINISHING

Hide yarn tails.

Block to the finished measurements.

Use mattress stitch to sew right shoulder seam.

NECKBAND

Using smaller needles and MC, with RS facing, pick up and knit 98 sts along neckline.

Work K2P2 Rib Pattern until the neckband measures approximately 1 in/2.5 cm from the beginning.

Change to CC, and work 1 more row in the pattern as established.

BO *loosely* in the pattern.

Use mattress stitch to sew the left shoulder seam, including the side of the neckband.

Sew in the sleeves. This garment has square indented armholes. Set in the sleeves, following the Assembly Illustration to ensure the perfect fit.

Sew the side and sleeve seams.

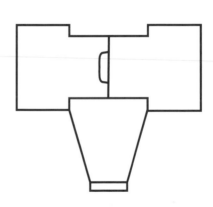

Assembly Illustration

Home Is Where the Heart Is

ADORABLE STUFFED HEARTS

You'll find lots of ways to use and display these cute stuffed hearts—assemble them in a pretty jar for a housewarming gift, or place them in a bowl as a decorative addition to your home. Each heart is made of two identical pieces, knitted in plain stockinette stitch from the lower point upward, and stuffed with fiberfill.

SKILL SET: *Cable cast on (page 20) • Knit stitch (page 21) • Purl stitch (page 24) • Kf&b increase (page 29) and M1 increase (page 29) • K2tog decrease (page 26), p2tog decrease (page 27), and ssk decrease (page 26) • Binding off (page 40) • Hiding yarn tails (page 48) • Blocking (page 44) • Mattress stitch seams (page 44)*

SIZE
One size

FINISHED MEASUREMENTS
Approximately 3 by 2¾ in/7.5 by 7 cm

YARN
» Yarn Sisters/Zealana *Willow DK* (3-light/
DK weight; 70% merino/30% cashmere;
140 yd/128 m per 1¾ oz/50 g): 1 ball makes
at least 3 hearts

Shown in Raspberry Wine, Silver Fern, Grey
Waru, and Natural

NEEDLES
US 6/4 mm knitting needles (or size needed to
obtain gauge)

NOTIONS
Blunt-end yarn needle

Fiberfill stuffing

GAUGE
20 stitches and 28 rows per 4 in/10 cm in St St,
blocked

To save time, take time to check gauge.

PATTERN NOTES
» Each heart is made of two identical pieces
worked from the bottom up, then seamed
together and stuffed.

» You can easily substitute yarns to use up
your odds and ends for this project. Be sure
to choose a small enough needle size that
will create a dense fabric so the stuffing
doesn't show through.

STITCH PATTERN
Stockinette Stitch (over any number of
stitches):

Row 1 (RS): Knit across.

Row 2: Purl across.

Repeat Rows 1 and 2 for the pattern.

BACK OF HEART

Use the cable cast-on technique to CO 2 sts.

BEGIN INCREASING

Row 1 (RS): Kf&b into each of the 2 sts—4 sts.

Row 2: P4.

Row 3: K1, kf&b into each of the next 2 sts, k1—6 sts.

Row 4: P6.

Row 5: K2, [M1, k2] twice—8 sts.

Row 6: P8.

Row 7: K2, M1, k4, M1, k2—10 sts.

Row 8: P10.

Row 9: K2, M1, k6, M1, k2—12 sts.

Row 10: P12.

Row 11: K2, M1, k8, M1, k2—14 sts.

Row 12: P14.

Row 13: K2, M1, k10, M1, k2—16 sts.

Row 14: P16.

Row 15: K2, M1, k12, M1, k2—18 sts.

Row 16: P18.

Row 17: K18.

Rows 18 and 19: As Rows 16 and 17.

Row 20: As Row 16.

SHAPE TOP

Row 21 (RS): K9, turn, leaving the rest of the row unworked.

FIRST SIDE

Row 22 (WS): P9.

Row 23: K2, ssk, k1, k2tog, k2, turn—7 sts.

Row 24: P2tog, p3, p2tog—5 sts.

Row 25: BO remaining sts.

SECOND SIDE

Row 21 (RS): With the RS facing, reattach the yarn to the next st, and k9.

Rows 22–25: Same as for first side.

FRONT OF HEART

Same as back.

FINISHING

Hide yarn tails.

Block to the desired size.

With WS of the pieces together, use mattress stitch to sew them together, stuffing the heart with the fiberfill as you go.

⊛ KNITTING KNOW-HOW

FULLY FASHIONED SHAPING

To make the seams easier and neater to sew, this project uses a technique called the fully fashioned shaping technique. In this technique, increases and decreases are worked away from the edge of the fabric (in this case, three stitches in from the edge). As a result, there are no lumps and bumps to deal with at the sides.

CHANGE IT UP!

Add dried lavender to the stuffing to create a scented sachet for your lingerie drawer.

Fair and Square

BUTTON-UP THROW PILLOW

This cool throw pillow is made from two knitted pieces sewn together perpendicularly to create visual interest. The pillow cover has a button closure for easy removal of the pillow form for laundering. The intriguing textured pattern is easily created with a two-row knit/ purl combination.

SKILL SET: *Cable cast on (page 20) • Knit stitch (page 21) • Purl stitch (page 24) • Binding off (page 40) • Picking up and knitting (page 42) • Hiding yarn tails (page 48) • Mattress stitch seams (page 44)*

SIZE
One size

FINISHED MEASUREMENTS
Approximately 16 in/40.5 cm square

YARN
» Cascade Yarns *Cascade 220* (4-medium/worsted; 100% wool; 220 yd/201 m per 3½ oz/100 g): 3 hanks

Shown in Mint #9076

NEEDLES
US 7/4.5 mm knitting needles (or size needed to obtain gauge)

NOTIONS
5 stitch markers

Blunt-end yarn needle

Five ⅞-in/2-cm buttons (shown with JHB International's Woods Hole #50813 in Burnt Wood)

16-in/40.5-cm square pillow form (available at your local craft or sewing store)

Sharp sewing needle

Matching sewing thread

GAUGE
20 stitches and 26 rows per 4 in/10 cm in the Garter Rib Pattern, blocked

To save time, take time to check gauge.

PATTERN NOTES
» This pillow cover is made in two pieces that are knitted together on the perpendicular.

» The buttonhole band is picked up and knitted later.

STITCH PATTERNS
Garter Rib Pattern (over a multiple of 4 sts + 2 sts):

Row 1 (RS): Knit across.

Row 2: *K2, p2; repeat from the * across, ending with k2.

Repeat Rows 1 and 2 for the pattern.

Garter Stitch Pattern (over any number of stitches):

Row 1 (RS): Knit across.

Pattern Row: As Row 1.

⊕ KNITTING KNOW-HOW

BUTTONHOLES
Don't let the buttonholes scare you—they're actually simple to make. For the buttonhole row, you will bind off a few stitches for each buttonhole. On the next row, just cast on the same number of stitches over the bound-off ones.

FIRST PILLOW PIECE

Using the cable cast-on technique, CO 82 sts.

Begin the Garter Rib Pattern, and work even until the piece measures approximately 17 in/43 cm from the beginning, ending with a WS row.

BO.

PERPENDICULAR PILLOW PIECE

With RS facing, pick up and knit 86 sts along one side edge of first pillow piece.

Begin the Garter Rib Pattern, and work even until the piece measures approximately 16 ½ in/42 cm from the beginning of the perpendicular pillow piece, ending after a WS row.

BUTTON BAND

Change to Garter Stitch Pattern and work even until the piece measures approximately 17¾ in/45 cm.

BO.

Place markers for 5 evenly spaced buttons on the button band.

BUTTONHOLE BAND

With the RS facing, pick up and knit 86 sts along the opposite edge of the first pillow piece.

Work in Garter Stitch Pattern until the band measures ¾ in/2 cm from the beginning.

Next Row: Knit across, making 5 buttonholes by binding off 4 sts opposite each marker.

Next Row: Knit across, using the cable cast-on technique to CO 4 sts above each set of bound-off sts in the previous row.

Work Garter Stitch Pattern until the band measures 1¼ in/3 cm from the beginning, ending after a RS row.

BO in the pattern.

FINISHING

Hide yarn tails.

Fold the pillow cover along the edge where you picked up stitches to begin the perpendicular piece. Fold the button band under the buttonhole band.

Use mattress stitch to sew the sides of the over-lapping garter stitch bands together. Sew the remaining sides of the pillow together.

Using the sharp needle and matching thread, sew on the buttons opposite the buttonholes.

Insert the pillow form through the opening.

CHANGE IT UP!

To knit a matching throw: Make 1 square as follows: CO 86 sts. Work in the Garter Rib Pattern until the piece measures approximately 17 in/ 43 cm from the beginning. BO. Repeat, to make 11 more squares. Sew the 12 squares together, making 3 strips of 4 squares each, alternating direction of rib for each one. Sew the strips together. Hide the yarn tails.

Looped

NECKLACE WITH A TWIST

This dramatic necklace is made using a technique called knitted idiot-cord (or i-cord, for short). Four stitches are knitted to create a narrow tube, and seven tubes comprise the piece. The applied bow is a fresh accent to the necklace, but it could easily be left out or made as a separate piece.

SKILL SET: *Cable cast on (page 20) • Knit stitch (page 21) • Binding off (page 40) • Hiding yarn tails (page 48)*

SIZE
One size

FINISHED MEASUREMENTS
Length: Approximately 36 in/91 cm

YARN
Classic Elite *Sanibel* (4-medium/worsted weight; 42% cotton/58% viscose; 125 yd/114 m per 1¾ oz/50 g): 2 balls MC, and 1 ball CC

Shown in Mouse #1306 [MC] and Verdigris #1346 [CC]

NEEDLES
Two US 7/4.5 mm double-pointed needles

NOTIONS
Blunt-end yarn needle

GAUGE
Gauge is not crucial to the success of this project.

STITCH PATTERN
Garter Stitch Pattern (over any number of stitches):

Row 1 (RS): Knit across.

Row Pattern: Knit across.

NECKLACE

Make 6 i-cords with MC and 1 i-cord with CC.

I-CORD

Use the cable cast-on technique to CO 4 sts onto one double-pointed needle.

Knit across the 4 sts.

*Slide the sts to the opposite end of the needle (where you began previous row).

Pull the working yarn tightly across the back, knit across the 4 sts.

Repeat from the * until the piece measures approximately 36 in/91.5 cm from the beginning.

Cut the yarn, leaving a 6-in/15-cm tail.

Thread the tail onto a blunt-end yarn needle, sew through the live stitches on the needle and pull the tail tightly.

Join the piece in a circle by sewing the first row to the last row.

FINISHING

On all seven i-cords, hide all yarn tails except for one. Use the remaining yarn tail to join all of the i-cords together. Hide remaining yarn tail.

CLOSURE

With CC, use the cable cast-on technique to CO 8 sts.

Work in Garter Stitch Pattern until the piece measures approximately 3 in/7.5 cm from the beginning.

BO.

Wrap the closure around all seven i-cord loops, covering the spot where you joined the pieces together. To secure the band in place, sew the edges together so they just meet, anchoring the band and the i-cords together.

DECORATIVE BOW

With CC, use the cable cast-on technique to CO 12 sts.

Work in Garter Stitch Pattern until the piece measures approximately 7 in/17.5 cm from the beginning.

BO.

Sew the cast-on and bound-off ends together.

CENTER OF BOW

With CC, use the cable cast-on technique to CO 4 sts.

Work in Garter Stitch Pattern until the piece measures approximately 2 in/5 cm from the beginning.

BO, leaving a 6-in/15-cm yarn tail.

Wrap the center of the bow around the bow. Thread the yarn tail from the center of the bow onto a blunt-end yarn needle, and sew the cast-on and bound-off edges together with the edges just meeting. Center the bow over the closure join, and sew in place.

KNITTING KNOW-HOW

WHEN GAUGE ISN'T CRUCIAL

Since this necklace is not meant to fit, this is one of those rare projects for which stitch gauge isn't crucial. Just grab two double-pointed needles in the suggested size, and you're off!

CHANGE IT UP!

For a matching bracelet, simply make shorter strands of i-cord.

All Is Welly

CUTESY BOOT TOPPERS

Knit these cute boot toppers to brighten a rainy day. They have a ribbed cuff to keep your calves warm no matter how wintry the weather.

SKILL SET: *Using double-pointed knitting needles (page 38) • Cable cast on (page 20) • Knit stitch (page 21) • Purl stitch (page 24) • Binding off (page 40) • Hiding yarn tails (page 48)*

SIZES

Women's Small/Medium (Large/Extra Large). Instructions are for the smaller size, with changes for the larger size noted in parentheses as necessary.

FINISHED MEASUREMENTS

Circumference at lower edge: 12(14) in/ 30.5(35.5) cm

Circumference at upper cuff: 16(18½) in/ 40.5(47) cm

Length (cuffed): 9½ in/24 cm

YARN

» Brown Sheep *Lanaloft Bulky* (5-bulky weight; 100% wool; 160 yd/146 m per 7 oz/200 g): 2 hanks

Shown in Lemon Pound Cake #LL-57

NEEDLES

1 set of 5 US 11/8 mm double-pointed knitting needles, or size needed to obtain gauge

NOTIONS

Blunt-end yarn needle

Two 1¼-in/3-cm buttons (shown with JHB International's Boise Style #48580)

Sharp sewing needle

Matching sewing thread

GAUGE

16 stitches and 20 rounds per 4 in/10 cm in the K2P2 Rib Pattern, unblocked

12 stitches and 20 rows per 4 in/10 cm in the Box Stitch Pattern, unblocked

To save time, take time to check gauge.

PATTERN NOTE

Each boot topper is knitted from the bottom up.

STITCH PATTERNS

K2P2 Rib Pattern (over a multiple of 4 sts):

Rnd 1 (RS): *K2, p2; repeat from the * around.

Pattern Rnd: As Rnd 1.

Box Stitch Pattern Worked in the Round (over a multiple of 4 sts):

Rnd 1 (RS): *P2, k2; repeat from the * around.

Rnd 2: As Rnd 1.

Rnd 3: *K2, p2; repeat from the * around.

Rnd 4: As Rnd 3.

Repeat Rnds 1–4 for the pattern.

Box Stitch Pattern Worked Flat (over a multiple of 4 sts):

Row 1 (RS): *K2, p2; repeat from the * across.

Row 2 (WS): As Row 1.

Row 3: *P2, k2; repeat from the * across.

Row 4: As Row 3.

Repeat Rows 1 through 4 for the pattern.

◉ KNITTING KNOW-HOW

STRETCH

The cast-on and bound-off edges of knitted pieces are two places the fabric doesn't stretch. Many knitters use a larger size needle to cast on and bind off for this reason. For this project, be sure to cast on *loosely* to ensure a comfortable and stretchy lower edge.

RIGHT BOOT TOPPER

Use the cable cast-on technique to CO 48(56) sts. Place a marker for the beginning of the round. Join, being careful not to twist the stitches.

Begin the K2P2 Rib Pattern, and work even until the piece measures approximately 6 in/15 cm from the beginning, ending after a WS row.

BEGIN THE UPPER CUFF

Begin Box Stitch Pattern Worked in the Round, and continue even until you have completed 22 rnds of the Box Stitch Pattern, ending after Rnd 2 of the pattern.

Next Row (RS): CO 8 sts for the button flap, and begin Box Stitch Pattern worked flat—56(64) sts.

Continue even for 5 more rows.

Next Row (Buttonhole Row 1, RS): Work 3 sts in the pattern as established, BO the next 2 sts, continue the pattern as established across to the end of the row.

Next Row (Buttonhole Row 2): Work the pattern as established, using the cable cast-on technique to CO 2 sts over the bound-off sts of the previous row.

Work even for 8 more rows.

Repeat Buttonhole Rows 1 and 2 once more.

Continue even for 5 more rows.

BO *loosely*.

LEFT BOOT TOPPER

Same as for right boot topper to upper cuff.

BEGIN THE UPPER CUFF

Begin Box Stitch Pattern Worked in the Round, and continue even until you have completed 22 rnds of the Box Stitch Pattern, ending after Rnd 2 of the pattern.

Begin Box Stitch Pattern worked flat, and use the cable cast-on technique to CO 8 sts at the end of the first row—56(64) sts.

Continue even for 5 more rows.

Next Row (Buttonhole Row 1, RS): Work the pattern as established until 5 sts remain in the row, BO the next 2 sts, continue the pattern as established across to the end of the row.

Next Row (Buttonhole Row 2): Work the pattern as established, using the cable cast-on technique to cast on 2 sts over the bound-off sts of the previous row.

Continue even for 8 more rows.

Repeat Buttonhole Rows 1 and 2 once more.

Continue even for 5 more rows.

BO *loosely*.

FINISHING

Hide yarn tails.

Fold the Upper Cuff in half to the RS.

Using the sharp needle and matching thread, sew on the buttons opposite the buttonholes.

CHANGE IT UP!

For toasty leg warmers, omit the Box Stitch Pattern cuff, and knit the K2P2 Rib Pattern in the round until the desired length.

That's a Wrap!

RIBBED HEADBAND

This wide headband is perfect for chilly breezes—or even just for a bad hair day. It is made out of basic stockinette stitch framed with knitted-in ribbing. The leather button on the back makes it easy to slip on and off.

SKILL SET: *Cable cast on (page 20)* • *Knit stitch (page 21)* • *Purl stitch (page 24)* • *Kf&b increase (page 29) and M1 knitwise (page 29)* • *K2tog decrease (page 26) and ssk decrease (page 26)* • *Binding off (page 40)* • *Hiding yarn tails (page 48)* • *Blocking (page 44)*

SIZE
One size

FINISHED MEASUREMENTS
Approximately 4½ by 20½ in/11 by 52 cm

YARN
» Jade Sapphire *Mongolian Cashmere 6-Ply* (4-medium/worsted weight; 100% cashmere; 150 yd/137 m per 2 oz/55 g): 1 hank

Shown in Pinksicle #110

NEEDLES
Two US 7/4.5 mm knitting needles (or size needed to obtain gauge)

NOTIONS
One ⅞-in/2.3-cm button (shown with JHB International's *Leather-All* #60330 in Dark Brown)

2 stitch markers

Blunt-end yarn needle

Sharp sewing needle

Matching sewing thread

GAUGE
21 stitches and 28 rows per 4 in/10 cm in St St, blocked

To save time, take time to check gauge.

PATTERN NOTES
» This project is made from the button end to the buttonhole end.

» Don't let the length of this pattern intimidate you. Once you get going, you'll be doing things in a predictable way and you'll be able to follow the instructions with ease.

STITCH PATTERN
Stockinette Stitch Pattern (over any number of stitches):

Row 1 (RS): Knit across.

Row 2: Purl across.

Repeat Rows 1 and 2 for the pattern.

HEADBAND

Using the cable cast-on technique, CO 11 sts.

Row 1 (RS): *P1, k1; repeat from the * across, ending with p1.

Row 2: *K1, p1; repeat from the * across, ending with k1.

Rows 3–8: As Rows 1 and 2.

Row 9: [P1, k1] twice, p1, place a marker, kf&b, place a marker, [p1, k1] twice, p1—12 sts.

Row 10: [K1, p1] twice, k1, slip the marker, p2, slip the marker, [k1, p1] twice, k1.

Row 11: [P1, k1] twice, p1, slip the marker, M1 knitwise, k2, M1 knitwise, slip the marker, [p1, k1] twice, p1—14 sts.

Row 12: [K1, p1] twice, k1, slip the marker, p4, slip the marker, [k1, p1] twice, k1.

Row 13: [P1, k1] twice, p1, slip the marker, M1 knitwise, k4, M1 knitwise, slip the marker, [p1, k1] twice, p1—16 sts.

Row 14: [K1, p1] twice, k1, slip the marker, p6, slip the marker, [k1, p1] twice, k1.

Row 15: [P1, k1] twice, p1, slip the marker, M1 knitwise, k6, M1 knitwise, slip the marker, [p1, k1] twice, p1—18 sts.

Row 16: [K1, p1] twice, k1, slip the marker, p8, slip the marker, [k1, p1] twice, k1.

Row 17: [P1, k1] twice, p1, slip the marker, M1 knitwise, k8, M1 knitwise, slip the marker, [p1, k1] twice, p1—20 sts.

Row 18: [K1, p1] twice, k1, slip the marker, p10, slip the marker, [k1, p1] twice, k1.

Row 19: [P1, k1] twice, p1, slip the marker, M1 knitwise, k10, M1 knitwise, slip the marker, [p1, k1] twice, p1—22 sts.

Row 20: [K1, p1] twice, k1, slip the marker, p12, slip the marker, [k1, p1] twice, k1.

Row 21: [P1, k1] twice, p1, slip the marker, M1 knitwise, k12, M1 knitwise, slip the marker, [p1, k1] twice, p1—24 sts.

Row 22: [K1, p1] twice, k1, slip the marker, p14, slip the marker, [k1, p1] twice, k1.

Row 23: [P1, k1] twice, p1, slip the marker, M1 knitwise, k14, M1 knitwise, slip the marker, [p1, k1] twice, p1—26 sts.

Row 24: [K1, p1] twice, k1, slip the marker, p16, slip the marker, [k1, p1] twice, k1.

Row 25: [P1, k1] twice, p1, slip the marker, M1 knitwise, k16, M1 knitwise, slip the marker, [p1, k1] twice, p1—28 sts.

Row 26: [K1, p1] twice, k1, slip the marker, p18, slip the marker, [k1, p1] twice, k1.

Row 27: [P1, k1] twice, p1, slip the marker, k18, slip the marker, [p1, k1] twice, p1.

Rows 28–125: As Rows 26 and 27.

NOTE: *Use a row counter or tick marks to keep track of your rows. If you wish to change the length of your headband, do so here. Begin the shaping 4 in/10 cm short of your total desired length.*

Continued…

Row 126: As Row 26.

Row 127: [P1, k1] twice, p1, slip the marker, ssk, k14, k2tog, slip the marker, [p1, k1] twice, p1—26 sts.

Row 128: [K1, p1] twice, k1, slip the marker, p16, slip the marker, [k1, p1] twice, k1.

Row 129: [P1, k1] twice, p1, slip the marker, ssk, k12, k2tog, slip the marker, [p1, k1] twice, p1—24 sts.

Row 130: [K1, p1] twice, k1, slip the marker, p14, slip the marker, [k1, p1] twice, k1.

Row 131: [P1, k1] twice, p1, slip the marker, ssk, k10, k2tog, slip the marker, [p1, k1] twice, p1—22 sts.

Row 132: [K1, p1] twice, k1, slip the marker, p12, slip the marker, [k1, p1] twice, k1.

Row 133: [P1, k1] twice, p1, slip the marker, ssk, k8, k2tog, slip the marker, [p1, k1] twice, p1—20 sts.

Row 134: [K1, p1] twice, k1, slip the marker, p10, slip the marker, [k1, p1] twice, k1.

Row 135: [P1, k1] twice, p1, slip the marker, ssk, k6, k2tog, slip the marker, [p1, k1] twice, p1—18 sts.

Row 136: [K1, p1] twice, k1, slip the marker, p8, slip the marker, [k1, p1] twice, k1.

Row 137: [P1, k1] twice, p1, slip the marker, ssk, k4, k2tog, slip the marker, [p1, k1] twice, p1—16 sts.

Row 138: [K1, p1] twice, k1, slip the marker, p6, slip the marker, [k1, p1] twice, k1.

Row 139: [P1, k1] twice, p1, slip the marker, ssk, k2, k2tog, slip the marker, [p1, k1] twice, p1—14 sts.

Row 140: [K1, p1] twice, k1, slip the marker, p4, slip the marker, [k1, p1] twice, k1.

Row 141: [P1, k1] twice, p1, slip the marker, ssk, k2tog, slip the marker, [p1, k1] twice, p1—12 sts.

Row 142: [K1, p1] twice, k1, slip the marker, p2tog, slip the marker, [k1, p1] twice, k1—11 sts.

Rows 143–146: As Rows 1 and 2.

Row 147 (Buttonhole Row) (RS): [P1, k1] twice, BO the next 3 sts, [k1, p1] twice.

Row 148: [K1, p1] twice, use the cable cast-on technique to CO 3 sts, [p1, k1] twice.

Rows 149–152: As Rows 1 and 2.

BO *loosely* in the pattern.

FINISHING

Hide yarn tails.

Block to the finished measurements.

Using the sharp needle and matching thread, sew on the button on end opposite the buttonhole.

CHANGE IT UP!

To make a dreamy eye mask, line the back of the piece with dark fabric, preferably a stretchy one. First, cut the fabric to size, allowing for 1/4-in/6-mm selvedges. Fold the selvedges to the wrong side and sew into place. I'd suggest using a flat button for the eye mask to make it comfortable while you sleep.

Forty Winks Throw

CABLED AFGHAN

The cable pattern in this blanket feels almost quiltlike. The stitch may appear to be complicated, but you really only have to pay attention on two out of the twelve pattern rows as you cross the cables. The superwash wool yarn is perfect for the project—as the name suggests, it's washable because it's been treated with a special process.

SKILL SET: *Cable cast on (page 20)* • *Knit stitch (page 21)* • *Purl stitch (page 24)* • *Cables (page 32)* • *M1 knitwise (page 29)* • *Binding off (page 40)* • *Hiding yarn tails (page 48)* • *Mattress stitch seams (page 44)* • *Picking up and knitting (page 42)*

SIZE
One size

FINISHED MEASUREMENTS
Approximately 54 by 70 in/137 by 178 cm, including border

YARN
» Cascade Yarns *220 Superwash* (3-light/DK weight; 100% superwash wool; 220 yd/201 m per 3½ oz/100 g): 22 balls

Shown in Alaska Sky #1914

NEEDLES
US 6/4 mm circular needle, 36-in/91-cm length (or size needed to obtain gauge)

US 4/3.5 mm circular needle, 36-in/91-cm length

NOTIONS
Cable needle

Blunt-end yarn needle

GAUGE
30 stitches and 30 rows per 4 in/10 cm in the Quilted Cable Pattern, blocked, with the larger needle

To save time, take time to check gauge.

PATTERN NOTES
» This blanket is knit in one piece; the border is picked up and knit on each side, then seamed at the corners.

» The circular knitting needle is used to accommodate the large number of stitches. Do not join the two ends; instead, work back and forth in rows.

STITCH PATTERNS
Quilted Cable Pattern (over a multiple of 18 sts + 2 sts):

Row 1 (RS): K4, *p3, k6, repeat from the * across to last 7 sts, p3, k4.

Row 2 and all WS rows: P4, *k3, p6; repeat from the * across to last 7 sts, k3, p4.

Row 3: K1, *slip the next 3 sts onto cn and hold in back, k3, p3 from the cn, k6, slip the next 3 sts onto cn and hold in front, p3, k3 from the cn; repeat from the * across to last st, k1.

Rows 5, 7, and 11: As Row 1.

Row 9: K4, *slip the next 3 sts onto cn and hold in front, p3, k3 from cn, slip the next 3 sts onto cn and hold in back, k3, p3 from the cn, k6; repeat from the * across, ending last repeat with k4 instead of k6.

Row 12: As Row 2.

Repeat Rows 1 through 12 for the pattern.

Garter Stitch Pattern (over any number of sts):

Row 1 (RS): Knit across.

Pattern Row: As Row 1.

BODY OF THROW

With the larger needle, use the cable cast-on technique to CO 380 sts.

Begin the Quilted Cable Pattern, and work even until the piece measures approximately 64 in/162.5 cm from the beginning, ending after Row 4 of the pattern.

BO in the pattern.

FINISHING

Hide yarn tails.

BORDER

With RS facing and using smaller needle, pick up and knit 263 sts along one short side of the throw.

Begin Garter Stitch Pattern, and use M1 knitwise technique to increase 1 stitch at each end every RS row 10 times—20 rows and 283 stitches total.

BO.

Repeat along the other short side.

With the RS facing and using smaller needle, pick up and knit 336 stitches along one long side of throw.

Complete the same as for the short side.

Repeat along the other long side.

With the RS facing, use mattress stitch to sew the corners together.

KNITTING KNOW-HOW

MEASURING GAUGE FOR CABLE STITCH PATTERN

It can be difficult to measure your gauge when working in some stitch patterns, especially cabled ones. Since you can't actually see every stitch to count them, measure across the width of one pattern repeat and divide. For example, at the gauge called for in this pattern, one 18-stitch repeat will measure 2¼ in/ 5.5 cm.

CHANGE IT UP!

Work the border in a contrasting color to match your décor.

Smitten Mittens

STRIPED MITTENS

Keep someone's hands (and heart) warm by knitting these mittens. They're made in the round from the cuff up in the softest wool imaginable. Stripes make them easy to customize for lucky folks on your gift list.

SKILL SET: *Using double-pointed knitting needles (page 38) • Cable cast on (page 20) • Knit stitch (page 21) • Purl stitch (page 24) • Attaching a new yarn ball (page 25) • M1 knitwise (page 29) • K2tog decrease (page 26) • Picking up and knitting (page 42) • Hiding yarn tails (page 48) • Blocking (page 44)*

SIZE

Average Women's(Men's). Instructions are for the smaller size, with changes for the other size noted in parentheses as necessary.

FINISHED MEASUREMENTS

Palm Circumference 8(9½) in/20(24) cm

Length: 11(12½) in/27.5(32) cm

YARN

» Manos del Uruguay *Maxima* (4-medium/worsted weight; 100% extra-fine merino wool; 219 yd/200 m per 3½ oz/100 g): 1 ball MC and 1 ball CC

Shown in Ion #2451 and Stratus #2426

NEEDLES

1 set of 5 US 6/4 mm double-pointed needles

1 set of 5 US 8/5 mm double-pointed needles, or size needed to obtain gauge

NOTIONS

3 stitch markers, one in a contrasting color for beginning of round

1 stitch holder

Blunt-end yarn needle

GAUGE

18 stitches and 26 rounds per 4 in/10 cm in the St St pattern worked in the round with the larger needles

To save time, take time to check gauge.

PATTERN NOTES

» The mittens are made from the bottom up in the round; the thumb is worked last.

» For ease in finishing, do not cut the yarn after each stripe; instead, carry it loosely up the wrong side of the fabric until it is needed again.

STITCH PATTERNS

K1P1 Rib Pattern Worked in the Round (over a multiple of 2 sts):

All Rnds: *K1, p1; repeat from the * around.

Stockinette Stitch Pattern Worked in the Round (over any number of sts):

All Rnds: Knit.

Stripe Pattern:

2 rounds MC, 2 rounds CC, [4 rounds MC, 2 rounds CC] twice.

✹ KNITTING KNOW-HOW

STRIPES AND COLORS

When you knit in the round and switch colors, you can see the color change at the "seam" where one row shifts to the next. To prevent this jog in the stripes, slip the first stitch of the second round of each stripe purlwise, then knit the rest of the stripe normally. This disguises the shift in color.

CHANGE IT UP!

For fingerless mitts, follow the pattern in a solid color, and stop the palm when the piece measures approximately 4½(6) in/11(15) cm from the beginning. Work in the K1P1 Rib Pattern for 1 in/2.5 cm, then bind off in the pattern. For the thumb, end after 1 in/2.5 cm, then work K1P1 Rib Pattern for 1 in/2.5 cm, and bind off in the pattern.

CUFF

With the smaller double-pointed needles and CC, use the cable cast-on technique to CO 34(40) sts. Place a marker for the beginning of the rnd. Join, being careful not to twist the sts.

Work 2 rnds of the K1P1 Rib Pattern.

Change to MC and knit 1 rnd.

Continue in K1P1 Rib Pattern with MC until the cuff measures approximately 3½(4) in/9(10) cm from the beginning.

Change to the larger double-pointed needles and work in Stockinette Stitch Pattern in the round with MC for 6(10) rnds ending 1 st before the end of the round; place a marker, k1, remove marker, k1, place a marker. There are 2 sts between the markers to begin the thumb gore.

BEGIN THUMB GORE

Next Rnd (Increase Rnd): Knit to first marker, slip the marker, M1 knitwise, work to next marker, M1 knitwise, slip the marker, knit to end of round—36(42) sts.

Repeat the Increase Rnd every other rnd 3(5) more times, then every 4 rnds once—44(54) sts with 12(16) thumb sts between the markers.

Knit 1 more rnd, ending when you reach the first marker.

SEPARATE THUMB FROM HAND

Remove the marker, slip the next 12(16) stitches onto a holder, remove the marker, and, using the working yarn and the cable cast-on technique to CO on 2 sts; place a marker for the new beginning of the rnd, then use the cable cast-on technique to CO 2 more sts and complete the rnd—36(42) sts. Turn so the RS is facing.

Work the 16-rnd Stripe Pattern once, then continue even in MC until the piece measures approximately 10(11½) in/25.5(29) cm from the beginning.

Next Rnd: Use the k2tog method to decrease 4(2) sts evenly spaced along the last rnd—32(40) sts remain.

DECREASE FOR MITTEN TIP

Next Rnd: *K2, k2tog; repeat from the * around—24(30) sts remain.

Work even for 1(2) rnds.

Next Rnd: *K1, k2tog; repeat from the * around—16(20) sts remain.

Work even for 1(2) rnds.

Next Rnd: *K2tog; repeat from the * around—8(10) sts remain.

Break the yarn, leaving 6-in/15-cm tail. Thread the tail through the remaining stitches and pull it snug to secure. Fasten off.

THUMB

Slip the 12(16) sts from the holder onto 2 double-pointed needles.

Using a third double-pointed needle and MC, pick up and knit 4 sts along the cast-on sts at thumb—16(20) sts.

Knit across the first 6(8) sts of thumb. This is now the beginning of the rnd.

Continue even for 2½(2¾) in/6(7) cm above the thumb cast-on stitches.

Next Rnd: Decrease 1(2) sts evenly spaced along the previous round—15(18) sts remain.

Next Rnd: *K1, k2tog; repeat from the * around—10(12) sts remain.

Next Rnd: *K2tog; repeat from the * around—5(6) sts remain.

Break the yarn, leaving a 6-in/15-cm tail. Thread the tail through the remaining stitches and pull it tight to secure. Fasten off.

FINISHING

Hide remaining yarn tails.

Block to the finished measurements.

Drop Everything

CAP SLEEVE PULLOVER

Made sideways from one side seam to the other, this elegant sweater is a breeze to knit. Dropped stitches provide a pretty design detail near the neckline.

SKILL SET: *Cable cast on (page 20)* • *Knit stitch (page 21)* • *Knitting a stitch through its back loop (page 73)* • *Yarn-over increase (page 27) and kf&b increase (page 29)* • *Purl stitch (page 24)* • *Binding off (page 40)* • *Ssk decrease (page 26)* • *Hiding yarn tails (page 48)* • *Blocking (page 44)* • *Mattress stitch seams (page 44)* • *Picking up and knitting (page 42)*

SIZES

Women's S(M, L, 1X, 2X, 3X). Instructions are for the smallest size, with changes for other sizes noted in parentheses as necessary.

FINISHED MEASUREMENTS

Bust: 36(40, 44, 48, 52, 56) in/91(102, 112, 122, 132, 142) cm

Length (including final edging): 25(25½, 26, 26½, 27, 27½) in/63.5(64.75, 66, 67, 68.5, 70) cm

YARN

Koigu *Kersti Crepe* (3-light/DK weight; 100% merino wool; 114 yd/104 m per 1¾ oz/50 g): 6(7, 8, 9, 9, 10) hanks

Shown in #K2424

NEEDLES

US 5/3.75 mm circular needle, 24-in/61-cm length

US 7/4.5 mm knitting needles (or size needed to obtain gauge)

NOTIONS

6 stitch markers

Blunt-end yarn needle

GAUGE

20 stitches and 28 rows per 4 in/10 cm in St St, blocked, with the larger needles

To save time, take time to check gauge.

PATTERN NOTES

» This sweater is knit sideways, from side seam to side seam.

» To ensure random color distribution, work from two different balls of yarn, alternating two rows from each.

» The circular knitting needle is used to accommodate the large number of stitches. Do not join the two ends; instead, work back and forth in rows.

STITCH PATTERNS

Stockinette Stitch Pattern (over any number of sts):

Row 1 (RS): Knit across.

Row 2 (WS): Purl across.

Repeat Rows 1 and 2 for the pattern.

K1P1 Rib Pattern (over a multiple of 2 sts):

Row 1 (RS): *K1, p1; repeat from the * across.

Pattern Row: As Row 1.

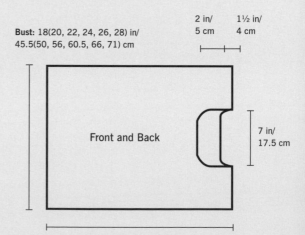

Bust: 18(20, 22, 24, 26, 28) in/ 45.5(50, 56, 60.5, 66, 71) cm

2 in/ 5 cm   1½ in/ 4 cm

Front and Back

7 in/ 17.5 cm

24(24½, 25, 25½, 26, 26½) in/ 60.5(62, 63.5, 64.75, 66, 67) cm

BACK

With the circular needle, use the cable cast-on technique to CO 120(124, 126, 128, 130, 134) sts.

Row 1 (RS): K21, [k1-tbl, place a marker, yarn over, place a marker, k1-tbl, k3] 3 times, k85(88, 90, 93, 95, 98) sts to end of row—124(127, 129, 132, 134, 137) sts.

Row 2: Purl across.

Row 3: K21, [k1-tbl, slip the marker, k1, slip the marker, k1-tbl, k3] 3 times, k85(88, 90, 93, 95, 98) sts to end of row.

Repeat the previous 2 rows 17(21, 23, 31, 35) more times.

Work Row 2 once more. You have worked 38(46, 60, 66, 74) total rows and the piece will measure approximately 4½(5½, 7¼, 8, 9) in/11(14, 18, 20, 22.75) cm from the beginning.

SHAPE NECK

Next Row (RS): BO 7 sts, continue the pattern as established across to end of row—117(120, 122, 125, 127, 130) sts remain.

Next Row: Purl across.

Next Row: Ssk to combine the first 2 sts, continue the pattern as established across to the end of the row—116(119, 121, 124, 126, 129) sts remain.

Continue even in the pattern as established for 43 rows.

Next Row (RS): Kf&b into the first st, work the pattern as established across to the end of the row—117(120, 122, 125, 127, 130) sts.

Next Row: Purl across.

Next Row: Use the cable cast-on technique to CO 7 sts, work the pattern as established across to the end of the row—124(127, 129, 132, 134, 137) sts.

Work even in the pattern as established for 37(45, 59, 65, 73) more rows.

⊛ KNITTING KNOW-HOW

OPENWORK

The yarn-over increases made in the first row of the knitting are later dropped to create the openwork. When unraveling those stitches, use the tip of a spare needle to gently unknit them.

Next Row (RS): BO, and, *at the same time*, drop the 3 single sts between the markers, and allow them to unravel down to Row 1.

FRONT

Work the same as the back until the beginning of the neck shaping.

SHAPE NECK

Next Row (RS): BO 14 sts, work the pattern as established across to the end of the row—110(113, 115, 118, 120, 123) sts remain.

Next Row: Purl across.

Next Row: Ssk to combine the first 2 sts, work the pattern as established across to the end of the row—109(112, 114, 117, 119, 122) sts remain.

Next Row: Purl across.

Next Row: Ssk to combine the first 2 sts, work the pattern as established across to the end of the row—108(111, 113, 116, 118, 121) sts remain.

Next Row: Purl across.

Next Row: Ssk to combine the first 2 sts, work the pattern as established across to the end of the row—107(110, 112, 115, 117, 120) sts remain.

Continued...

Next Row: Purl across.

Next Row: Ssk to combine the first 2 sts, work the pattern as established across to the end of the row—106(109, 111, 114, 116, 119) sts remain.

Continue even in the pattern as established for 35 rows.

Next Row (RS): Kf&b into the first st, work the pattern as established across to the end of the row—107(110, 112, 115, 117, 120) sts.

Next Row: Purl across.

Next Row (RS): Kf&b into the first st, work the pattern as established across to the end of the row—108(111, 113, 116, 118, 121) sts.

Next Row: Purl across.

Next Row (RS): Kf&b into the first st, work the pattern as established across to the end of the row—109(112, 114, 117, 119, 122) sts.

Next Row: Purl across.

Next Row (RS): Kf&b into the first st, work the pattern as established across to the end of the row—110(113, 115, 118, 120, 123) sts.

Next Row: Purl across.

Next Row: Use the cable cast-on technique to CO 14 sts, work the pattern as established across to the end of the row—124(127, 129, 132, 134, 137) sts.

Complete same as for back.

FINISHING

Hide yarn tails.

Block to finished measurements.

Use mattress stitch to sew the right shoulder seam.

NECKBAND

With RS facing and the straight needles, begin at the left front neck edge, and pick up and knit 114 sts along the neckline.

Work K1P1 Rib Pattern until the neckband measures approximately 1 in/2.5 cm from the beginning.

BO *loosely* in the pattern.

Use mattress stitch to sew the left shoulder seam, including the side of the neckband.

Place markers 8¼(8¾, 9, 9¼, 9¼, 9½) in/21(22, 22.75, 23.5, 23.5, 24) cm down from the shoulder seam on both the front and the back pieces on each side.

ARMBANDS

With RS facing and the straight needles, pick up and knit 66(70, 74, 78, 78, 82) sts between the markers on one armhole.

Begin K1P1 Rib Pattern, and work even for 1 in/2.5 cm.

BO *loosely* in the pattern.

Repeat for the other armhole.

BACK LOWER EDGING

With RS facing and the straight needles, pick up and knit 100(108, 116, 124, 132, 140) sts along the lower edge of the back.

Begin K1P1 Rib Pattern, and work even for 1 in/2.5 cm.

BO *loosely* in the pattern.

FRONT LOWER EDGING

Work the same as the back lower edging.

Sew side seams, including the sides of the lower edging.

CHANGE IT UP!

For a solid sweater without the open-work, just follow the directions but omit the yarn overs on the first row and the dropped stitches when binding off.

Under Wraps

LACY RECTANGULAR SHAWL

This cozy rectangular shawl offers the perfect canvas for trying out new stitch patterns. This one is knit in a variation of a traditional lace pattern called feather and fan. The four-row repeat is simple to memorize, so you'll get the hang of it quickly.

SKILL SET: *Cable cast on (page 20)* • *Knit stitch (page 21)* • *K2tog decrease (page 26) and ssk decrease (page 26)* • *Yarn-over increase (page 27)* • *Purl stitch (page 24)* • *Binding off (page 40)* • *Hiding yarn tails (page 48)* • *Blocking (page 44)*

SIZE
One size

FINISHED MEASUREMENTS
Approximately 24 by 75 in/60.5 by 190.5 cm

YARN
» Classic Elite *Magnolia* (3-light/DK weight; 70% merino wool/30% silk; 120 yd/110 m per 1¾ oz/50 g): 13 balls

Shown in Bisque #5406

NEEDLES
US 7/4.5 mm circular needle, 24-in/61-cm length (or size needed to obtain gauge)

NOTIONS
Blunt-end yarn needle

GAUGE
22 stitches and 28 rows per 4 in/10 cm in the Lace Pattern, blocked

To save time, take time to check gauge.

PATTERN NOTES
» This shawl is worked side to side.

» The circular knitting needle is used to accommodate the large number of stitches. Do not join at the end of rows; instead, work back and forth in rows.

STITCH PATTERN
Lace Pattern (over a multiple of 11 sts):

Row 1 (RS): *[K2tog] twice, [yarn over, k1] 3 times, yarn over, [ssk] twice; repeat from the * across.

Rows 2 and 3: Knit across.

Row 4: Purl across.

Repeat Rows 1 through 4 for the pattern.

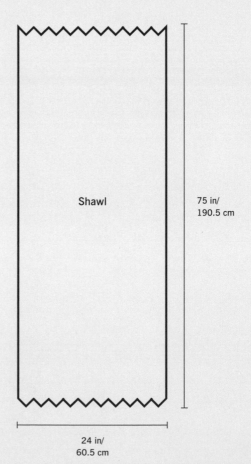

Shawl

75 in/
190.5 cm

24 in/
60.5 cm

SHAWL

Use the cable cast-on technique to CO 132 sts.

Begin the Lace Pattern, and work even until the piece measures approximately 75 in/190.5 cm from the beginning, ending after Row 1 of the pattern.

Next Row (WS): Knit as you BO.

FINISHING

Hide yarn tails.

Block to the finished measurements.

✹ KNITTING KNOW-HOW

Don't let the brackets in Row 1 of the lace pattern throw you. The brackets just mean to repeat whatever is bracketed for the number of times specified. Here's how to read the row stitch by stitch: K2tog, k2tog, yarn over, k1, yarn over, k1, yarn over, k1, yarn over, ssk, ssk. Then, repeat the whole thing to the end of the row—with 132 stitches, you'll have 12 repetitions of the pattern. Some people like to put stitch markers between each pattern repeat, which can make it easier to see where you've added or subtracted a stitch and correct your error. Others prefer to just "read" their stitches and not fuss with markers. If you find that you are struggling with this pattern, see if markers help you.

CHANGE IT UP!

To make a perfect-size afghan, cast on 275 stitches and knit until the piece measures approximately 68 in/173 cm from the beginning, ending after Row 1 of the pattern. Then bind off as described in the pattern. Keep in mind you'll need more yarn to knit an entire afghan than a wrap, but for a knitter, there's no such thing as too much yarn!

PART 3: RESOURCES

MATERIALS

I always recommend purchasing your yarn and other materials from your local yarn shop. If there isn't one in your area, contact the appropriate wholesaler below for help locating one.

Brown Sheep Company
www.brownsheep.com

Cascade Yarns
www.cascadeyarns.com

Classic Elite Yarns
www.classiceliteyarns.com

Fairmount Fibers
fairmountfibers.com

Jade Sapphire
www.jadesapphire.com

JHB International, Inc.
www.buttons.com

Knit Collage
www.knitcollage.com

Koigu Yarn
www.koigu.com

Lion Brand Yarn
www.lionbrand.com

Malabrigo Yarn
www.malabrigoyarn.com

Manos del Uruguay Yarn
(*see* Fairmount Fibers, left)

Miss Babs Yarn
www.missbabs.com

Plymouth Yarn Company
www.plymouthyarn.com

Rowan Yarn
(*see* Westminster Fibers, below)

Westminster Fibers
www.westminsterfibers.com

Yarn Sisters
www.theyarnsisters.com

Zealana Yarns
(*see* Yarn Sisters, above)

BOOKS

To expand your knowledge of knitting, take a look at the following books. There's so much to learn and explore!

Hiatt, June Hemmons. *The Principles of Knitting*, 2nd ed. New York: Simon and Schuster, 2011.

> This encyclopedic book includes nearly every technique a knitter would need to look up—and more.

Kooler, Donna. *Donna Kooler's Encyclopedia of Knitting*, Revised ed. Little Rock, AR: Leisure Arts, 2012.

> This volume contains technical information as well as several projects to knit, from lace to cables, and beyond.

Melville, Sally. *The Knit Stitch*. Sioux Falls, SD: XRX Books, 2002.

> This book is a great introduction to the basic knit stitch and includes several interesting projects for beginners.

Melville, Sally. *The Purl Stitch*. Sioux Falls, SD: XRX Books, 2003.

> The second volume of Melville's *Knitting Experience Series* introduces the purl stitch and explores the wonders of stockinette stitch fabric.

Newton, Deborah. *Designing Knitwear*. Newtown, CT: Taunton Press, 1998.

> This book provides a fascinating glimpse inside the brilliant creative mind of one of the country's most exciting handknitting designers.

Vogue Knitting eds. *Vogue Knitting: The Ultimate Knitting Book*. New York: Pantheon, 1989.

> The definitive guide to all the basics of knitting, this book was written by the editors of one of the most loved magazines in the fashion industry.

RECENT TITLES BY AUTHOR MELISSA LEAPMAN

Cables Untangled. New York: Random House/ Potter Craft, 2006.

> Written to be the indispensible guide to cable knitting, this book includes basic how-to material, an inspirational cable stitch pattern dictionary, and fun projects for women, men, kids, and the home.

Color Knitting the Easy Way. New York: Random House/Potter Craft, 2010.

> This book focuses on color knitting techniques that use just one color per row, including stripes, slip stitch knitting, tuck stitches, mitered squares, and more.

Continuous Cables. New York: Random House/ Potter Craft, 2008.

> Another of the author's cable knitting books, this volume offers a complete study of cables that have circular elements to them—Celtic knots, curliques, and rings.

Knitting the Perfect Fit. New York: Random House/Potter Craft, 2012.

> A designer's guide to shaping your knits, this book is a complete workshop on using fully fashioned shaping to flatter the figure, no matter the body type.

Mastering Color Knitting. New York: Random House/Potter Craft, 2010.

> The second of the author's books about color knitting, this volume focuses on advanced techniques such as intarsia, stranded fair isle, and two-color double knitting.

Stashbuster Knits. New York: Random House/ Potter Craft, 2011.

> All knitters seem to accumulate lots (and lots) of yarn, and this book offers suggestions on organizing, storing, and using that yarn to create fun projects for women, men, kids, and the home.

The Knit Stitch Pattern Handbook. New York: Random House/Potter Craft, 2013.

> The author compiles 300 of her favorite stitch patterns from cables to lace to slip stitch textures and more in this handy resource.

KNITTING COMMUNITY

To learn more about the craft of knitting and to meet other enthusiastic knitters, turn to one of the following resources:

THE KNITTING GUILD ASSOCIATION

Check out this wonderful nonprofit organization to find a local group of knitters. They even sponsor exciting events with classes, vendor markets, and more!

www.tkga.com

RAVELRY

To meet other knitters online, visit Ravelry, a vibrant website where you can keep track of all your projects, search for designs you might like to make, and share your knowledge and love of knitting. To keep up with me and my work, join my fan group, "Melissa Leapman Rocks," started by one of my fans.

www.ravelry.com

INDEX